"E1

British Indian"

Sarinder Joshua Duroch with his wife Suneeta

"Enoch,
I am a
British Indian"

From the rupee to the euro with a
double-headed coin?

Sarinder Joshua Duroch

THE CHOIR PRESS

First published in the United Kingdom in 2014 by
The Choir Press

ISBN 978-1-909300-50-7

For Neelam Duroch,
my dear sister who is no longer with us. You were my first
friend and my loving sister; I will always miss you.

Contents

Acknowledgements

A significant amount of thought has gone into writing this book; it would not have been possible without the Scottish education that I was exposed to and the knowledge that was shared with me by the early British Commonwealth citizens who settled in the great city of Glasgow.

My grandparents on both maternal and paternal sides of the family deserve thanks and praise from me for all that they shared relating to their experiences in the nation of Britain, which I love with all of my heart. This nation for them, as immigrants from the Commonwealth, was a new home that they truly accepted, embraced and loved on many fronts; that embrace faced many difficulties before I could truly lock myself in the vision that they had for future generations.

My parents in particular deserve thanks for being able to put up with the lengthy debates that I subjected them to in my teens and early twenties, although my father enjoyed those debates; he always stated that he saw his own father through me. My father in fact contributed to these debates, as he clearly enjoyed being a news addict and at dinner times he would discuss the daily events with me. I owe him a lot for this because it really did allow me to mature quicker than most who fell into my age group.

The city of Glasgow is at the epicentre of my thanks; this city gave me more than I could ever give back to it. My home city prepared me for life and gave me a social education that has always stayed with me. The diverse nature of the city, due to its heritage and relationship with the world through its former industries, has contributed towards my inquisitive nature. The teachers of the city are a great gift to this nation and to me personally, as they were always instrumental in developing my thought process and most of all contributed towards my socialisation process.

The open-minded thinkers of our nation who have a sense of pride relating to Britain's present and future status must be thanked; there are many of them whom I know personally, but sadly they sometimes do not get heard. I must thank a good friend, Matt Ashton; he is one of the true Englishmen that I have met who really does know how to debate and offer solutions. He always said, 'if we keep on making this nation too attractive we will be adding to our existing problems drawing its attention to those who wish to take advantage of our nation.' I would also like to express my gratitude to my friend Robert Morris who inspired me to embrace faith and contribute towards open-minded debate and dialogue; his wisdom relating to politics, sociology and theological debate is simply superb and most of all it is very encouraging to know that I can always talk to him about the vision for our nation from a unified perspective. Robert and I spent many nights discussing the issues surrounding our nation and I will always be thankful to my friend for being there to support me and my cognisance.

At home I have to give the biggest thanks to my wife and children for putting up with my social and political views. Regardless of how much I can debate and discuss issues of concern, these people in my life will always remain a source of peaceful equilibrium between me and the wider society that I live within. Suneeta, who is my dear wife, has had to listen to hours of social and political debate and I do wonder how she had the patience; it truly must be love, or her patience threshold!

Last but not least I want to thank my children for being so wonderful to me and my wife. They truly have been instrumental in all that I do in life; I do it for them and I hope they grow to love this nation as much as I do.

CHAPTER ONE

Introduction to My Early Socialisation Process

I was born in the west end of Glasgow in Redlands Hospital in 1973. My father was a west-end man and my mother came from the south side. This in itself was a social contrast, and my dear mother particularly felt the differences; she was born in Galashiels in the south of Scotland during rationing after the war, so Glasgow in effect was her second home. I myself am still very proud to have been born in the city that was known as the second city of the British Empire.

In the west end of the city there are beautiful buildings and beautiful parks, and my time there as a child up to the age of six was a very pleasant part of my life. I attended Renfrew Street Nursery School and later Garnetbank Primary School; this is where I was first introduced to a society of people who were friendly and very cosmopolitan. Being based in the centre of Glasgow had huge advantages, especially for a young child who was always desperate to go to the famous Sauchiehall Street to visit a toy shop known as the Walrus and Carpenter. I was just another child of the city and I remember that at that young age I was very proud to encounter hackney cab drivers taking disabled kids out for the day. How can I ever forget seeing those taxis and the decorations that were attached to them? I was very touched at the age of six years to see this beautiful gesture of charity that my city's people had implemented for the benefit of the disabled kids. I was very pleased to see this level of humanity and heart; it made me feel proud to be part of my city.

By the time I was eight years old we had moved to the south side of the city; for me this was a new world altogether. However, one advantage was being around a new set of kids who were really friendly towards me; they became like a new family for me and they did their best not to make me feel any different. I had neighbours in the tenement block and the most charismatic were Pamela Steele and her brother Alan. They would always take me around the area on a bicycle and play with me in the street. It is fair to say that I became very attached to Tracy and Sandy Maberly, who lived opposite me on the same landing. We lived in the famous Waverley Gardens and at that time it was known as a really nice part of Shawlands. My socialisation process was in the embryonic stages but there were not many electronic distractions, so all we really had was each other to be with.

The wonderful part of this early stage of my socialisation process was that I was the only brown person that these people really knew! Tracy would take me to school and Sandy would be the one whom we relied on to help out if other kids tried to annoy us, because he was bigger than the rest of us. The colour of my skin was not an issue to me or my early social circle; in fact it is fair to say that I was just another little Glaswegian who had just as much to offer the circle of mischief as anyone else in the street. One thing we all had in common was music. We loved it! I really believe that this created a cohesion that forged us into one epicentre of friendship and the equilibrium between us was just unique. I was no dancer, but the girls could dance and at every opportunity they would enjoy music and dance. We as boys just liked the music and not the dancing. I will never forget the time when Alan Steele helped me to tape a transistor radio onto my bicycle: a huge techno-logical advancement at the age of six!

When I got to my new school I soon realised that football was not all that it seemed. I was asked whether I was Rangers or Celtic, but I had no comprehension or understanding of any rivalry; I had never really been exposed to it. I was about eight years old and all I could hear around the playground was boys conducting verbal commentary as they dribbled the ball around. It soon became apparent that there was a divide between groups; this divide became more apparent amongst the white kids in the school. I still could not see colour; I could only see people and for me that was what mattered.

I was approached by a mixed-race lad who was very popular for bad behaviour. His dad owned a shop just off Minard Road in Shawlands and we all knew his family because there were so many of them. His mother was a Scottish Christian and his father was a Pakistani Muslim, yet he too was consumed with the culture of division between Celtic and Rangers. His approach towards me was dictated by the need to ascertain some key information for his team selection, a team that was expected to play football in snow and ice; most participants only came out with injuries. He asked me if I was a Proddie or Catholic; I clearly did not know what this meant so I asked him to explain it. He said, 'Are you Rangers or Celtic?' as he stood there with a clenched fist; it felt like that scene out of the movie *The Deer Hunter* where the Vietnamese got the Americans to play Russian Roulette. I gambled and said, 'Celtic is my team.' A big hug followed and then I was placed in goal to pass my induction. What a predicament to be placed in at a young age, being faced with one's fate in the form of a physical attack over faith and football.

I then clearly remember my first experience of trouble at the school. The same boy had a fight over Rangers and Celtic in the boys' toilets; by chance I was there. He kicked down a door in the toilets and it was amazing to watch this spectacle. Like the rest, I made a dash for the playground. I had not done anything, but the next day an investigation was conducted and the opposing team of Rangers supporters went off and said that I was the one who was behind this performance of mischief. The only description that they could give was that it was a brown kid. Later I was taken to the headmaster's office and I was given a hiding for something that I did not do. All the headmaster kept saying was, 'I was told it was you. Stop telling fibs; it was you, boy!' After trying to explain my innocence, all I got was a hiding. At the age of eight, this was my introduction to being at the wrong end of the stadium that was filled like a cauldron of hate. I was really annoyed at not getting a fair hearing. I remember going to tell the other kids, and to my astonishment they felt very sorry for me. I promised myself that I would always fight for my justice in life after that episode. I did see the headmaster in Shawlands one day and I walked up to him and told him I was innocent. The look on his face was of shock that a little kid still would not let this issue rest. He told me to go to Woolworths and spend my pocket money on sweets. I suppose his conscience played on his mind, but at the end of the day I was right and he was wrong.

The whole thing was over football and religious perception. I have to use the word 'perception' because the study of theology could not really be comprehended by a group of young Glaswegian kids in the early 1980s, so it had to be a social perception that dictated the conduct of kids at a young age.

I knew there was a divide and rivalry. This was my first introduction to segregation, and I do not hold any anger towards the people of my city but I do question the nature of the link between football and faith, which in my humble opinion does not have any place in society, particularly not in Glasgow; oh no, not in Glasgow. I must say, though, that before an Old Firm match the speculation created an atmosphere that was electric; sadly it just had the wrong theme attached to it, and that still does upset me each time I visit my city.

It did give me an insight into social perspectives by the time I got to secondary school. This was where I really learned about friendship, authority and of course religious divides as well as multi-ethnic divisions. My first day at secondary school was really good; I was very proud to be attending one of the better schools in the city, and at that time it was known to be a good seat of learning. I joined in the academic year 1984–85. I was really taken by surprise by the facilities that were available to the kids; we had a swimming pool, a language lab, a good English department and most of all space. The place was huge, the playing field was enormous and to be honest with myself I felt proud to be part of this environment. I remember meeting some kids from Sir John Maxwell Primary School; they were hard Rangers supporters, and they had no real issue with me until they discovered that I was a Celtic supporter. Once again I could see this division brewing in the kettle when all I wanted was refreshment and a rest from that nonsense.

My socialisation process in the school reached fruition in the Modern Studies department; I believe it is appropriate to call it a political science environment. My teacher was Mr Miller, who was very tall indeed but a friendly giant who would really engage in dialogue. I will never forget the sessions that we had relating to South Africa and the terrible apartheid regime, to communism and of course to our very own UK political system of government. I still remember what he taught me and I am proud to say I have managed to share this knowledge with my own children. I started to relate the sectarian divide in my city to the apartheid regime in my mind and it helped me to understand the structure of division. I was about thirteen or fourteen years old and this for me was the perfect age to move on to the next stage of my socialisation process. We had hardly any African or Afro-Caribbean communities in Glasgow, so for me the study of apartheid was an amazing way to learn about the outside world and the divisions that were placed within it.

Mr Miller was the architect of explanation; he explained apartheid to me by getting a white boy to sit with me, then explaining that we would not be able to do this in South Africa and stating the reasons why. I must say his explanations relating to the single transferable vote and proportional representation required a bit more in-depth analysis; however, on the subject of apartheid he was very good in the ways in which he made the lesson very interesting. I used to leave the class and check all my possessions to ensure that nothing was from South Africa because I believed I had a duty to contribute towards sanctions in my own little way.

I will never forget the time when this really hit hard in my early teenage years; my maternal grandfather, along with my uncle, came up with this idea to buy a fruit and vegetable shop. I only mentioned South African fruit to my grandfather and he hit the roof, saying, 'We do not buy anything from those racist bastards!' I personally did not know who sounded more angry, my grandfather or the South African regime.

A white Scottish customer in the shop said, 'Too right; we have nothing to do with those racist, arrogant and ignorant bastards!'

I got told off for even bringing the topic up, but I did ask the customer something very intriguing indeed; I asked him outright, 'If the South Africans are so bad then why are so many of our own Scots over there profiting from a system that is so wrong?'

He just looked at me and said, 'What, are you working for some newspaper? You've got to remember, wee man, us Scots are the friendliest in the world towards people.'

It was at that point that I realised that there was something not right about division in society, especially along racial lines.

Enoch Powell was once interviewed and asked about race; he stated that he did not focus on race or make it an issue. At this point in my life he was a man whom I saw as the one who was responsible for making the lives of my grandparents difficult in this nation, so at that age he made no impact on my school of thought. In fact I was petrified of his appearance because he had a similar look and style to the very same head-master at Shawlands Primary who gave me a hiding.

It became apparent during my school years that the shape of the country was not all that the Conservatives were making it out to be. The IRA were still a major force who were giving the Conservatives hell as far as I was concerned, but the loss of life even at that age hurt me. It was never off the news and if something happened one would hear the anti-Catholic taunts in the playground. 'No surrender to the IRA and to the Fenians!' The fights after school and horrible statements about the Pope were not good at all for the image of our school, and all of this was happening because certain people wanted to capitalise on someone else's sorrow. I stopped a few of the fights but I could never change minds; that was not really my intention, but it would have helped if back in the day our school had done more to change this school of thought.

Although it was a time of perceived economic prosperity, nowhere in my city could I see anyone who resembled my ethnicity working in a public sector job, so I soon started to relate what I was being taught in Modern Studies to what was happening around me in the city of Glasgow. I did know this much: that Mrs Thatcher was public enemy number one in Glasgow, so the school of thought from any Conservative really was not welcome in our public or domestic domains.

In the '80s there was no internet, so all I could do was go to the library and seek knowledge from there. I approached an old man in Govanhill Library and I asked him if he was happy in Glasgow; he responded by asking me, 'Why do you ask, son?' I persisted and he told me that he was happy, but that happiness was one of the hardest things to find in society. He also stated that he could only see the poor getting poorer. Well, he was not wrong about that!

A lot was happening at the time, especially around the Live Aid project. For once many people saw not colour or race but the suffering of children in Ethiopia; this really moved so many people at the time. I am very proud that our nation gave so much. For once in my school there was no divide about the issue, but there was some unity of thought surrounding human suffering. It was all funded by the people of this nation, so it connected us to people in another nation who were suffering. Nowadays I am more worried about whether the money is getting to the right people. I even ask myself the question now of whether it is our responsibility to resolve the issues of other countries; at times I do wonder indeed.

With so much happening around the world at the time, one may ask how any young person could pay attention to a lot of what was going on. The answer is simple: I wanted a social education and I went out to get one. It was not so easy, but it had to be achieved.

I will never forget the time when Margaret Thatcher came to present the Scottish Cup to the winning Celtic team and our captain, Roy Aitken, went to receive the trophy from her. All one could hear was the booing and hissing towards this one person. I was close to Hampden that day, our national stadium, and I will never forget the hatred of words that I heard from the Celtic faithful. I just could not believe how much a prime minister could be hated by so many.

Later that year I went to Kent to visit some cousins and they were not so against the school of thought surrounding the Conservatives. I could clearly see the amount of money that the Tories spent in areas that voted for them; I knew then that life can be corrupt and that if one votes in the right direction one will be rewarded in some context. In the sense of infrastructure it was evident that Kent had better roads than my home city and more wealth amongst the upper classes. I saw a different society from my school, city and social circle; there were black people and many people of Asian origin, and of course there were no sectarian issues. I did notice, though, that there were more racial divisions rather than religious ones. I myself felt that the large numbers of Asians and black people in the south of the nation was something that would take me time to adjust to, because back home in Glasgow the social structure was so different. Even as a teenager I could see that Britain was not a multicultural society because all I saw in the south of the nation were racial divisions and areas where there were not many indigenous white people, yet we were all being made aware of this 'multicultural society'.

I returned to Glasgow and I met a good friend of mine named Phil; his dad is an Englishman from the North of England. I went to visit him and that is where I heard the perception of England from an Englishman for the first time. Phil's father said, 'How was your trip to Kent, son?' I told him that I did not see many white people but lots of Asians and black people. He smiled and said, 'Well, now you know how it feels where there are so many of them, and I am no racist but why do you think I came here to Glasgow, mate?' I knew that he felt no animosity towards me but he went on to say, 'Enoch was right but sadly our people always criticise the truth; what is right is wrong and what is wrong is right!' It made me think, it really did, and I knew then that there was not only a divide in my city but also a divide in my nation.

I left their home knowing that it would be very unfair to call him a racist man, which I knew he truly was not. I jumped on the number 57 bus to Govanhill and a turbaned Sikh was driving. I did not pay the correct fare and another Asian man came on board who happened to be the inspector; he approached me and told me to get off the bus because the fare had increased. I was not best pleased but he chucked me off the bus in a vocal manner. As the bus driver looked at me I said, 'Just like Gandhi being thrown off the train in South Africa; bloody joke how your own treat you!' I went on to say, 'Who gave the both of you jobs anyway?' An elderly Glaswegian was at the bus stop and he said, 'You sound more white than me, son.' I didn't mean to sound like a prejudiced person but I soon realised if I had been white the bus staff would have taken it as racial. So as a result of that day I realised that knowing is not enough; we must apply more knowledge to support the statements that we make in society. This incident opened my mind, not in full, but enough to question society and false claims of prejudices from my own society, who assumed rather than engaging to ascertain the true feelings of someone who was being misunderstood.

Reflecting on what I had said relating to MK Gandhi, I

visited the library and read a book about this great man; it really did educate me to the extent to which I could relate my ethnicity to this man who believed in non-violence and freedom. It soon became a reality to me that without independence there is no choice. I based a lot of my thought processes on the struggle that this great Indian had to go through. It also came as a surprise and an eye-opener to me that when he visited Britain in the early 1930s he was very much loved by the British working people he met. It gave me an insight into how great the British people can be when it comes to sharing a common bond of freedom, especially when the enemies are imperialists and greed. By making himself a common man amongst the people he managed to relate to the peoples of Great Britain and India. I must admit that I really believe that Enoch Powell and Gandhi were two great speakers of the English language and both loved their own nations and the ethos of freedom. It is very thought-provoking that both made speeches for the benefit of their respective nations, but one of them left a legacy that is only now being revisited through the present status of Britain and its place in Europe.

As a young man in Glasgow I came across a lot of people of Irish origin who really disliked Winston Churchill but loved MK Gandhi. Intrigued by this mystery, I tried to ascertain the source of this love and respect many of them had for such a great man. I had a friend in Kirkintilloch, a town on the outskirts of Glasgow, and his father was the one who told me why the Irish had an affinity with MK Gandhi; the answer was simply freedom and the struggle for it from the British Empire. I then realised that my own ethnicity was something to be proud of and not something just to be overlooked. Surely, just as Phil's dad felt proud of Enoch Powell, this in turn gave me the right to have a role model who clearly was someone whose name echoed through hearts, minds and nations. It also became more evident to me that no wonder there was a sectarian divide in my city; it was purely down to history and bigotry. However, the divide still puzzled me considering that, although India suffered under the colonial rule, somehow MK Gandhi and Mountbatten managed to forge a bond of friendship that enabled Britain and India to have sound links today. Mountbatten had great respect for MK Gandhi; he insisted on calling him 'Bapu', which means 'father'. Consider that Mountbatten was from a royal family; one would think that there is no way that a royal could make friends with someone who clearly was trying to end British rule in his nation. This friendship also enabled me to have an open mind and look deeper into the prospect of linking the two great cultures together through my own socialisation process, in which I knew had a lot to learn; why not look at white people with the view of finding a common bond that was not just about football but of humility?

The only problem that I encountered was that there were many stereotypes in Glasgow. Regardless of how British I saw myself as, I was only given two options back home in Glasgow, and those were Scottish or Indian. I was not ethnically Scottish and I was not an Indian national, so where did I stand? I saw myself as Scottish when it came to supporting our national football team but British in terms of nationality. This was thrown back in my face by a boy named Colin who attended Shawlands Academy; we were in the sports department and he had an issue with some of the boys of Pakistani origin. Somehow he reached the conclusion that I should not be in this country because it was his country and I was someone who was not meant to be there. I did respond, by saying to him that I could not change my colour but I was British. He responded by saying, 'Oh, you are British, then, you wee bastard? Well, you are still foreign; get out of Scotland!' The PE teacher heard it and gave him a proper ear bashing. I was told by the teacher that I should be proud to be British because of the efforts of the Indian soldiers during the war. I felt that this was not the only social and political qualification that was required to be British; the fact that I had a British passport, a very strong Glaswegian accent at the time and a love for the museums of Glasgow were also contributing factors. I believe I referred to the museums because they represented my home city, of which I was obviously a strong part.

It became apparent to me that people like Colin hated most people. It was only a few days later that he approached me in the freezing snow and told me to behave in school, otherwise people would think I was English. This made me smile at his stupidity. It was only a year later that he discovered that his very own mother was English. That soon became public knowledge throughout the school, and then it was he who became the victim of racism from other white kids. He started to call himself British after that; how strange that he took a leaf out of my book to define his national status.

It was the summer of 1988 and Glasgow had a famous festival, the Glasgow Garden Festival; this was a huge highlight in the city and the authorities welcomed children from schools to visit this great splendour. As if we had a desire to learn about plants! We all went to the festival on the banks of the River Clyde and it was a great day for me and for the entire year group.

There was a funny incident where there was a group of black kids from London and one of them caught the attention of a man on stilts. The man approached the black kid and insisted on touching his hair; it was light-hearted fun because the man said that he wanted the same style for his own hair but in Scottish ginger. This caused a lot of dismay amongst the Londoners, but as for us we didn't find it to be racial or nasty; as we saw it, it was just part of the Glasgow humour. However, one of the Londoners was not happy and he complained about it to a policeman who was wandering around. To be honest I found this to be really silly because there was never going to be an arrest over that sort of thing happening. The Londoner got told by the Glasgow policeman to get a grip on himself before the policeman gripped him; he meant it and walked off.

All I heard from the white teacher from London was, 'Oh God, they are so backward here; look at how they treat black people.' I found this to be pathetic at the age of fourteen. One must realise that to call someone 'coloured' back home when I was young was just a natural thing to do; there were no boxes that had to be ticked to categorise oneself, so to me I was coloured and different in terms of appearance. This came to my disadvantage years later when working in Wild Street just off Covent Garden in the centre of London. I asked a youth worker if he had any white people on his caseload or just coloured people; the guy hit the roof in anger. I thought he was going to throw me out of the building! He responded angrily by saying, 'No, no, no, in London if you are black you are just that and if you are of Asian origin then you are just that; none of us are coloured, have you got that, Jock?'

I responded with a touch of humour, 'Thanks for the race relations lecture, mate, but hey, is it only Jocks who get branded the same regardless of colour?' That soon shut up his political correctness mindset.

Although I was a typical Glaswegian lad I was aware of my own Indian culture and I made regular visits to the Sikh temple with my parents. On a Sunday that was where all the families met and caught up with community affairs; it was also where I attended to learn Punjabi. I just could not see what I was doing there at the time because as far as I was concerned I attended mainstream school and that was enough; it is only in later years that one realises that education is beneficial. One of the female teachers was very strict and she made it clear that there were many white people who could speak Hindi and Punjabi because of the British Empire, so we too should make an effort to learn our mother tongue.

I was hit with this reality many years later when I had a full discussion in Hindi with an Englishman who had been born and brought up in India; the contrast was like a mirror reflecting back at me and him because he felt that India was his home and not Britain, and I on the other hand looked at Britain as

my home and not India. It was a moment of social education
that could only lead to an open-minded way of thinking; it was
at times like this that I could see a link forged between the two
nations. However, I could only really have had this encounter
in England, because during the British Empire there were far
more English than Scottish out in India.

When I was in Glasgow I discovered that there were small
areas where Asians would live; places like Govanhill and
Pollokshields had a lot of Asians living there, so in those areas
one felt safe from racial abuse. The only problem was that
India and Pakistan never got on with each other, so it really
depended on what side of the border you came from. I will
never forget this boy of Indian origin whose dad owned a shop
in Govanhill; the son was of the Sikh faith and he was terribly
racist towards Pakistanis. He told me off for talking to Pakistanis one day and then he kicked me for supporting Celtic
because he was a Rangers supporter. I did kick him back, but it
truly was a case of taking the horse to the water but being
unable to make it drink. That episode makes me think of the
scene in Shakespeare's *Macbeth* where the three witches are
stirring the cauldron of hate with a wooden spoon. The spoon
is being stirred in a circle that has only one side: the dark side
of a city that has been created by its history, and which can be
changed only if its people can be enlightened by open minds.

It was at this point that I started to seek out the other side of
cultural and religious divides. It was now getting closer to home
because I knew that Indians and Pakistanis did not always get
on, so who were the real bigots: the Rangers and Celtic supporters, the general majority white public of the city, or people who
were the same in colour as me? It soon became apparent that it
was not a black and white issue but a lot deeper than that.

Enoch Powell mentioned civil war; this always scared me
because my own grandparents suffered the civil war relating to
the partition of India between Muslims, Sikhs and Hindus.
The horrors that they witnessed and endured were beyond
belief; however, I was living amongst the descendants of the

perpetrators of that civil unrest from both communities, and it was a strange thought to know that I could in effect be safer in a white community because there was no religious hatred to find there in me or them. I was of Sikh faith back then; I was no Catholic or Protestant, so what did I have to worry about? **I converted my faith and became a Christian Roman Catholic in 2011**; I suppose now I have become a Glaswegian with an identity, if one can see the humorous side of my statement.

When given the category of British Asian, one may not necessarily feel safe within that category; was I not better off being part of a uniculture instead of being a crash test dummy for the new emerging ethos of multiculturalism? Being at school was enough for me to have a foundation for where I wanted to be politically, but in Glasgow it was all really Labour and that was the path that most followed. I did not see any need to celebrate multiculturalism as a youngster because, to be honest with myself, I was still trying to embrace the good things about Scottish culture in and around the city. That was more essential for me because my future and life were destined to be British and remain British, so why on earth would I want to be anything else?

In my later teens I saw the emergence of this new multiculturalism at my local college and even then I saw no need to force anyone to learn about my ethnic culture; it was actually being enforced on people by political correctness. I remember going into my local library and hearing a young lad ask for 'the yellow peril'. This was the Glasgow City Council vacancy list; it was always on yellow paper and you would apply at your own peril. The manager rushed over and told the young boy off for saying 'the yellow peril' because it was offensive to Chinese people. I must give the guy credit because he did say that he had never had any complaints from a Chinese person and he went on to insist that he would consider any complaints that had been made in writing by a Chinese person. This was my introduction to the mass confusion of identity that I believe we have in our nation today.

CHAPTER TWO

A Visit to India – Introduction to Social Apartheid

In October 1988 I visited India and I was really excited about meeting family that I had never met before. I had to get a visa for the country from the High Commission in Glasgow and I was really made to feel like a foreigner by people who shared the same ethnicity as me. I was a free man in Britain, regardless of being a minority, but I could not enter India without a visa.

It came to me as a huge surprise when I got to India; the security and immigration police personnel at the airport were so rude it was beyond belief. They could not understand that I had just been issued with a new red EU-style British passport. The Indian police had taken over the immigration booths because at the time they had a massive problem with civil unrest in the Punjab and this show of strength was meant to be a contributing factor to dealing with the problem.

It was a right performance. The officer looked at the passport and could not work out what country it came from; I had to explain to the fool that it was British and the last time I checked they stayed in India for a good 150 years, so why could he not recognise the words 'United Kingdom of Great Britain and Northern Ireland'? Eventually a so-called senior officer came along and reached the conclusion that I was from a small island named Dublin so I was OK. What a performance indeed! I was amazed at this spectacle, mainly due to the rudeness and the display of authority even when one is blatantly wrong.

I must admit there was a lot I strongly loved about India and there was a lot I really hated about the place. I was amazed that the average Indian just could not access health care, and the sanitation was beyond belief. I must say the corrupt rich had it all but the average poor person would be left to die if they had no money to save themselves.

I met an Indian doctor in a village and he mentioned that so many doctors worked in the British NHS who were of Indian origin. I agreed with his point; it is of course very true. He then mentioned to me that I must have experienced racism in Britain. I looked at him in surprise because I wondered why this should concern him, and most Indians believe that Asians have no problems over here. He chuckled and mentioned Enoch Powell: 'What a strange man he is, you know; on one hand he invited Indian doctors to work for the NHS and on the other hand he changed his mind about Indian people and stopped them from going to the UK.'

I responded in a very serious manner: 'If he had an issue with Indians, then why did he respect the educated ones who clearly had something to offer our country Great Britain?'

The doctor questioned my statement with surprise. 'Your Britain, you say? They allow you to call it your country, do they?'

It was at this point that I realised that I must be unique in my thought process; was it only I who viewed Britain in this way? At the age of fifteen going on sixteen one begins to believe that he or she is the most misunderstood person, even without the social wrangling to add to the dilemma of growing up.

As a young man Enoch went to India and worked in the intelligence section of the Indian Army, and he fell in love with the place; he was actually in awe of India. He once said, 'I fell head over heels in love with it. If I had gone there 100 years earlier I would have left my bones there.' This is the opposite impression to a lot of British Indians who are third- or fourth-generation British; I have seen some out there on holiday who do not adapt and want to get back to Britain so that they can get back to the pub to watch their football team.

People would look at me as 'the foreigner'; they could tell by my clothing and my mode of social interaction that I was different. I made a friend over there and he was illiterate but very good at kite making and kite flying. He lived next door to us and he was known as Kashmira. One day I spoke to him about all the stares that I was getting; he said, 'Why don't you wear Indian clothing, mate, and nobody will know the difference? You are the one who is making yourself stand out.' I paused and thought about the statement he had made for a while, and then I asked myself a question: Asians in Britain wore their own native dress and nobody stared at them, so why was I being told to change my clothing? I presented this to him and he said, 'Our people are not right in the head, mate; I heard it is a cold country, your Britain is, so why do our people insist on wearing Indian clothing but when you come here you wear British clothing?' I laughed at this because he was more practical than me in his way of seeing culture and I was looking at the sociological side of life. He became a really good friend of mine, but he always knew I was not a true Indian but one who had come to see his roots. For hours upon end he tried to teach me cricket; he and his family would always have a laugh over the concept of Britain creating the game but India being so much better at it. I stood no chance against him or the village kids but I did manage to translate a lot of the rules for them; the only difference was they knew that if you just hit the ball hard and go for a six you will win the game regardless of the rules.

I asked him why he did not attend school and he told me that he did not stand much of a chance in life because he was of low caste. This was an issue that I was aware of; caste discrimination was and still is a terrible curse on Indian society. In rural India and in many urban cases it is a form of social apartheid that clearly discriminates in employment, marriage, village life and social status. My friend went on to say, 'What chance have I got, mate? I will still be known as a leather shoe maker's son in the damn school and they will make me sit on the floor there, with the high-caste teachers being in charge of discriminating against us.' I was sickened by this statement; back home in Britain we were all equal in that sense and we had no social apartheid, so for me this became an education that had a sense of reality to it.

'Let's face it, mate,' he said, 'you speak English so well you could make them all look stupid in that school if I took you there, but they will also see you as a low-caste person.' Well, at that point the Glaswegian kiss came into my mind, so I came up with the idea of going to the school to nut those bigots. He told me that if I did that the police would torture so many low-caste people it would end up causing civil unrest in the place. He did ask for a demonstration of the Glasgow kiss, then he tried to head butt a buffalo that only pissed all over him on his first attempt. The laughter was immense and he said, 'You are lucky; in Glasgow you can do a Glasgow kiss without being pissed on by the local wildlife.'

Being the person I am, I still went to the school to talk to the headmaster; my uncle took me along. The headmaster knew my uncle, so he was on friendly terms, and he asked me if I was able to speak to a class in English; I agreed. I will never forget a boy of higher caste in the class whispering to the lad next to him, saying, 'He is an educated low-caste one they have; he is the British one.' I asked him if he knew the birthplace of MK Gandhi and the teacher was very eager for him to answer; one of the kids asked me if I knew, so I told him that it was in the state of Gujarat, Porbandhar. They were all amazed that I knew. I told them I was allowed to learn back home without caste, colour or race being an issue. They could not comprehend this because it was a new concept to them, but I did leave knowing that it was one-nil to Great Britain. The teacher looked at me and recommended that I do teaching one day as a profession; now that was one positive omen he gave me. In later years I took his advice.

As the months progressed I began to see so many social divisions that were based on social status; at times it was disgusting to see how children of the lower castes were being treated by higher castes in the place. I would see the lower-caste children begging for food and being made to work in child labour conditions that were beyond belief. I would talk about this to my family but they accepted it because they too, like most, surrendered to the ethos of this cruel system of social apartheid. As a young man I would see the injustice, and when I added up all the figures I realised that India had managed to import a terrible caste-discrimination social apartheid system into Britain through immigration. I was not wrong to think like this because the reality was in front of my eyes. My friend was amazed that I had so much knowledge about caste, coming from Britain; this really took him by surprise. He told his elder brother and he even stated that it was sad that Indians managed to export this terrible system of apartheid into Britain. It was actually his dad who told me that if too many Indians went to Britain it would not be a good idea because it would only result in everybody being deported. I found this to be extreme but he did have a point that too much immigration into a small nation is not good at all. He did admire the British. I asked him why; he responded in a very funny tone, 'We fought for our independence and objected to them being here in our land, yet they liked us so much they still let a lot of Indians into Britain.' I laughed it off and told him that economics had a lot to do with the restructuring of Britain after the war and cheap labour was required. He just looked at me, smiled and said, 'Remember too much of anything is not good, and that includes your famous Scottish whisky, OK?'

As time went on I discovered that people from different lands are much the same with interaction, and curiosity seemed to add to the welcome that I got from most people. In those days the telecommunications in India were really bad; I will never forget having to travel over an hour to get to a government telecommunications office. It was Christmas Day and I just had to call my family back in Glasgow to wish them a Merry Christmas. We always celebrated Christmas and for once I was not at home back in Glasgow, so I really felt lonely at the age of fifteen. There were no presents or decorations around so it just felt like a normal day; I dearly missed my own country at this time in my life. A week later it was New Year's Eve and that was beyond belief! Everybody went to sleep early and the next morning nobody even wished each other a Happy New Year. In Scotland Hogmanay is a massive event as we all know. I couldn't believe that I was the only one wishing people a Happy New Year and the people were just looking at me as if I was some alien.

The state of Punjab was not in a healthy position; the Indian government had sent thousands of troops into the state to restore calm due to the uprising that had happened four years earlier in the city of Amritsar. As many will know Mrs Indira Gandhi was assassinated over the whole affair and this caused a major backlash against the Sikhs of the nation. Wherever I went all I saw were armoured personnel carriers and soldiers all over the place.

I will never forget being in a bus that was shot at; some of the bullets missed, but some did hit the near side. The driver kept going until he reached a safe haven. An Indian soldier appeared and requested that everyone get off the bus so they could be checked; his mannerisms were not so good, but then again he was not so aggressive. He came up to me and as soon as he saw my appearance he knew that I was not Indian born and brought up.

'What is that you are wearing?' he asked me in a very inquisitive manner.

'It is my football team's shirt,' I responded in a happy manner for some reason that is still beyond me, because this officer took everything the wrong way in his mode of thinking.

'Green and white are the colours of Pakistan; are you lying to me?'

I was lucky; in the centenary year of Celtic Football Club, 1988, the club had introduced the Gaelic cross rather than the traditional Irish clover. When he saw the cross he knew that it was a Christian symbol, so he eased his manner of questioning. I gave him my passport and he checked it all out and then instructed me to get in the armoured personnel carrier. I thought I was going to be taken to some torture centre, but a senior officer insisted that I be taken home because they could not risk something happening to a foreigner. They dropped me off near my home and then shook my hand and told me that it was safer in Britain and that I should go back there. It was a strange experience in the personnel carrier because all I heard the other soldiers saying was that they too wanted to return to their home state and never come back to Punjab. For once I felt as if I was not the only outsider in such a huge country and it was reassuring to know that I was not the only one who missed home.

As each day went by I learned about society and how it worked in India. I used to go to the town centre on my own a lot even though it was not advisable. I would get stopped, checked and then let go as usual. I always kept my passport on me as protection in case there was a problem.

One day I was in the city of Hoshiarpur and I started to chat with a shopkeeper about history for some reason. He directed me to a place in Hoshiarpur that I will never forget in my life; it is called the Shish Mahal. It means 'palace of glass', although I must admit I did not see much in the way of glass because it all needed a good clean. It was spectacular. An Indian artist, Jan Mohammad, depicted a coronation ceremony all from his own imagination; he recreated the coronation of King George V in the form of statues. The place was not well maintained but for me it was a place of amazement. Britain had accidentally just got closer to me that afternoon; it all had a feel to it that was like being back in a Glasgow museum. An Indian actually felt it was his duty to recreate this scene in the form of statues; that is an amazing thought to embark upon.

It was then that I started to conduct a search around the city for other architectural likenesses of Britain; whatever old building I could find, I would ask the occupants or the government officers about its history. I went to the old court room in Hoshiarpur and I was told by a police officer that the building was built by the British because it was always a British judge who sat in court and he was normally the main person in the town at the time. I could really see the historical link between Britain and India because all the procedures looked the same but for the corruption, and that is where we British have the upper hand, although some readers of this book would raise an eyebrow at what I have just written.

I soon realised that this culture seemed to be one that did engage with the world rather well; one only needs to look at the contribution that India has made to literature, mathematics and medicine, to say the least. I gained a lot of respect for my ethnicity that afternoon in the Shish Mahal through the work of the artist, but it did feel like I was being reminded that I am a citizen of two different worlds. Then again, Rudyard Kipling did say, 'East is East and West is West'. When one engages with the intricate details of the social structure of Indian life then one can only agree that this is a very true statement.

I was walking down the street looking for some shade because it was very hot that afternoon; to my surprise I ended up seeing a dead body being carried through the streets on a makeshift stretcher with loads of flowers and incense. I was intrigued by the fact that nothing seems to be hidden in this nation and all seems to be in the open, but when one is alive one has to hide one's caste in order to get up the social ladder or have a chance of not being discriminated against. However, in death one can be carried through the streets and people will pray with hands clasped as the body is carried past, regardless of caste or social class. It was very thought-provoking for me because Enoch's famous words flashed back into my mind. Why on earth did he say, 'It is like watching a nation busily

engaged in heaping up its own funeral pyre' when we all know most if not all Indians conduct funeral ceremonies by cremation and this is normally done with the construction of a sandalwood funeral pyre? This occasion reminded me of the link between Indian traditions and the words Enoch used to complain about 50,000 immigrants entering the country each year back in the '60s. One can imagine how the Indian immigrants at the time could have related this comment to their cultural practice. I soon realised how well constructed the speech was; even though I did not agree with certain words that he used, it was none the less well thought out with the intention of creating a storm. It was strange to stand there as a fifteen-year-old youth watching all of this and remembering my own nation being portrayed in the words of Powell as a funeral pyre. One can relate to this if one is a deep thinker to begin with. I spent the afternoon drinking Campa Cola and watching life go past me, and all the time I just found myself being critical of certain things that I could see in front of my eyes like the child labour and the terrible driving standards.

I was sitting comfortably in a shop and some college girls came in and all they did was giggle at me for some reason; I believe it was my very short haircut and the fact that I had headphones on. I was a bit annoyed at them, and then one of them asked me if I was from Delhi.

'Delhi? Nah, not me; I am from Glasgow.'

The girls just stared at me because I approached them as if they were inferior to me, although that was not my intention. They were still laughing and giggling at my short hairstyle. One of the girls, who had brightly coloured clothing on and books held so close to her chest one would think she was scared that I would steal them, asked, 'Where in India is Glasgow?'

I could not believe what she had just said. I replied, 'Glasgow is in Scotland, the United Kingdom.'

She seemed a bit more comfortable with this and then she concluded the probing session by saying, 'Oh, yes, Scotland is a lovely part of England; my dad drinks their whisky.'

I could not believe what I was hearing, so I spent the next hour explaining to her and her friends what the difference was. I believe they were insulted when I reminded them that Britain and the Empire had ruled them for so long one would think they would have learned something from them. The same girl dipped her eyes and replied, 'When they were here all they ever did was stay in their clubs; no dogs or Indians were allowed in the places where they congregated.' It was at this point that I sympathised with her because I shared the same ethnicity as her, so I could share the feeling of degradation. She did say that I would be better off becoming a teacher because she could see that sort of trait in me, but I did not see that coming in my life until a few years later.

I managed to export a very traditional British schoolboy playground game to the children: conkers. What better way is there for any young lad to spend the afternoon? We had merchants who came to the village to sell Kashmiri walnuts. I was taken by surprise because I had never really seen people who looked like them: different dress, striking looks and of course another dialect that I had to get used to for a brief twenty minutes of buying and selling. I thought that they were Brahmins, the highest caste of Hindus; my uncle told me that they were Muslim people and that was why they entered into our part of the village, because they did not have the same caste segregation rules. I bought the walnuts and could not find anything to open them, so I got my shoelace and made a string of conkers. This was the big new invention as far as the local kids were concerned; the next thing I knew, people would bring their kids to learn about this new game that came from Britain. I was really happy that I gave them something to do to pass the time. My friend Kashmira was annoyed because nobody would jump on his roof and conduct kite flying sessions; he gave up and joined us eventually.

The following week it just poured down and sadly I got caught in the torrential rain. Just outside the village there were armed soldiers guarding a school because that week the assassins of Mrs Indira Gandhi were due to be hanged, so one can only imagine the tension that was in the air. One of the guards jumped down from the roof of the school and pointed his machine gun at me and shouted, 'Oi, are you the foreigner from Britain?' I nearly fell off my bike with the shock of an armed guard running towards me with this weapon. He told me he had something to show me, so I let him explain what he had in his weapon carrier. 'I have got this shoelace from my other boots and I have walnuts; I want you to show me and my commanding officer how to play this game.'

This was one massive relief. 'You guys really know how to scare seven shades of shit out of someone, don't you just?' That was my response of relief, and believe me it was relief, although it was not the fear of being slapped and told off that created the relief; I was more afraid of being locked up on some false charge that they felt like creating to pass the time. India is so corrupt that this can happen, followed by days of torture and in some cases family members being taken into custody and brutally beaten even if they have nothing to do with the situation.

I spent the next hour in the rain explaining the rules to the soldiers in English, because they could speak the language really well and it was always a pleasure to speak English again. I did ask the guard why he approached me in the manner in which he did; he smiled and said, 'Look, mate, we have been trying to find you for a week. If we'd called you over you would have cycled away in fear, so we had to stop you so we could learn how to play this famous game.'

For once during my time in India, caste, politics and social apartheid did not get in the way and I soon realised that in life we all need a distraction to get away from the not-so-nice aspects of society, both in India and here in Britain. It was very funny for me because I just could not comprehend what all the fuss was about, but the local kids did not have much, so for them this was a big thing and an exciting new game to play. The only problem was each time the walnut seller came into the village I was expected to buy the same kids walnuts, so I struck a deal, and that was that each time the nut cracked they would have to bring the walnut for me and my closest friends. Simple all of this may well be to the Western child, but for them it was something that brought them closer to me.

I will give them credit where it is due: when I helped the kids with English, their desire to learn was far greater than anything I had seen in Britain. I brought this ethic of learning back to Britain with me and it has always stayed with me. Even when they had electricity blackouts they would light a candle and still study; that is something that would not really happen here. The thirst for academic knowledge over there is a delight to watch, and it is no surprise that education and the principles of it are given very high regard in the average Indian or British Indian household.

The children who are from the scheduled castes (the ones who are known as the untouchables) are amongst the highest academic achievers in India, especially those who are given opportunity; this has been more evident during the last twenty-five years. An example of this achievement could be seen back in 1997 when KR Narayanan became India's first Dalit president; **a Dalit is someone who is known as a suppressed or broken-to-pieces person, a trodden-on person, a member of the scheduled castes.** Another great Indian, Dr Bhimrao Ambedkar, became a law minister within the newly formed Indian government. As independent India's first law minister, he was the writer of the famous Constitution of India. As someone who came from a Dalit caste he fought for the rights of those who were of the deprived castes, and he fought for the abolition of untouchability and introduced civil liberties for those who were deprived of rights in society. Although not publicised as much as his passion for pursuing the rights of those who were from a Dalit background, he is also known for his struggle to gain economic and social rights for women. He ensured that those who were previously discriminated against would in law be given equality of opportunity in both social and professional fields. I am very proud as a British national that this man came to the United Kingdom and became a barrister; he chose to study at Gray's Inn in London and he enrolled at the London School of Economics where he embarked upon a doctoral thesis. I do ask the question of how hard it must have been for this man to return with so much academic attainment to India, where he was still considered to be a Dalit and part of an oppressed caste within society.

The Sachar Committee Report of 2006 compiled by the National Sample Survey Office (NSSO), a branch of the Ministry of Statistics in India, disclosed some interesting figures. It was highlighted that scheduled castes were not just confined to Hinduism but also included members of other faiths in India. These traits have been exported to Britain through the immigration of the '50s and '60s.

The proportion of members of different faiths who belong to the scheduled castes in India:

Buddhism	**90%**
Christianity	**9%**
Sikhism	**31%**
Hinduism	**22%**
Islam	**0.8%**

It is reported that nearly 17% of the population of India is from the scheduled castes; however in the state of Punjab it is reported that the figure is as high as 29%. I would like to add that there are many people in British towns and cities who are of Punjabi origin.

In Punjab the land owners in general have always had a tradition of being wealthy and having lower-caste people working for them in their fields whilst they sat on horseback and watched the slave labour for their economic advantage in action. This has changed a lot in recent years due to the rise of scheduled-caste children progressing up the academic ranks in order to get away from the tyranny of working for higher-caste land owners. I must say that from my experience and observation caste discrimination is still rife in the Punjab but the brutal implementation is not as evident as in other states; the landowners in other states who happen to be of higher caste do tend to be a lot crueller towards the lower castes.

I was at the well one day just watching the water being extracted to irrigate the local fields. To be honest I was just waiting for an opportunity to jump in the naturally made pool, but I soon stopped when I saw a snake slithering around; I am still petrified of these evil creatures. All of a sudden this high-caste woman came along and grabbed a young man and said to him, 'Oi, you low-caste bastard, just because the two of my sons had a punch-up what right did that give your low-caste people to spread the news around the village?'

I was sickened by this approach because evidence for all that I had learned about the caste system and the social apartheid ethos had just appeared in front of me. The poor man explained to her that he was so sorry on behalf of his low-caste community and begged forgiveness from her. I approached him and I just had to let my anger out. I looked at her, although I was talking to him; my eyes were raging and I said, 'What the hell are you doing asking her for forgiveness? Do you not have any sense of dignity?'

I will never forget the woman's words echoing in the narrow village alleyway. 'Ah, you have a lot to learn about people, young boy; those white people have been treating you so nicely. Speak all the clever English you want; to me you will always be the leather shoe maker's son!'

To me this statement was disgusting considering that her stepson used to come to our home to learn how to read and write from my uncles and grandfather. My paternal grandfather was a school teacher and a very politically minded man; he held a lot of respect due to his job and he was also a very stubborn man who believed in his political views. I am sure that is why she said what she did, because she could never accept that her own high-caste landowners were all illiterate and had no need to get an education. This incident stayed in my mind for a long time in life and it urged me to look into life a lot more when interacting with people of the same ethnicity as me; on most occasions it was proven that caste is still a major problem in the Indian communities in India and worldwide.

I was wandering around the city centre one day and this policeman walked into a sign-writing shop to have his rifle's number repainted as it had worn out. It was very hot, and he mentioned that he could do with a cold drink to kill his thirst; I asked for water and the owner gave me a freezing cold bottle of mineral water. The policeman noticed that the shop had a painting of a scheduled-caste saint on the wall. I just looked at his expression; he was so disappointed that he could not drink from that shop because it was owned by lower-caste people. I watched him go across and buy a bottle of mineral water from another shop, and then he came back to pick up his rifle. I mentioned it to the shop owner; he was not as surprised as me because it was common practice over there to do such a thing. He said, 'Oh, you will leave this nation soon and you must tell the British about this social apartheid and racism we encounter every day. Just imagine if he had arrested me; he would have beaten me up and then they would have been so cruel to me because of my caste.'

At this point I just wanted to see the Union Jack and the white cliffs of Dover. I knew we were not perfect with race relations, but I am sure Enoch Powell would not have refused medical treatment from an Indian doctor just because he was from a different race. He did once say during the famous *Frost on Friday* interview, 'It is the fear and increase of the large numbers of immigrants.' In India there was a similar sentiment in the fear of the Dravidians, who were the indigenous population of India who watched the Aryans coming into the land; these Aryans were responsible for implementing an apartheid system.

In Enoch's Britain most people had freedom, but for the new Commonwealth immigrants there was little equality and in some instances the denial of dignity. These three elements – freedom, equality, dignity – are at the core of the ethos of independence for an individual, group or whole nation and there should be a suitable equilibrium between all three. Enoch made his speech in 1968; now, forty years and a little more since then, we are very much ahead of others within Europe in implementing all three core elements. Surely this is something we must celebrate to its maximum potential. One would think that my ethnicity, having come from such a civilised and advanced race, would have exported this three-pronged approach to the rest of the world; sadly it did not, but I took that ethos with me to India in 1988 and I noticed how great a favour Britain had done me in looking at democracy, freedom and dignity. I must admit everyone around me looked like me in terms of ethnic features, but I was faced with a new challenge; I always saw people in Glasgow and not colour, but in India, where I was trying to implement the same ethics, sadly everyone was looking at me as a caste and not as a person. I was exposed to a new form of racism that was really cruel. Even the people who wanted change and better rights had to stay within their own caste to feel protected, thus causing a continuous vicious circle.

I was studying some speeches that I got hold of relating to Enoch Powell many years later, and I applied one of his statements to what I had witnessed as a young man out there on a visit to the land of my ethnicity. He answered one of Frost's questions really well. Frost asked the critical question, 'A lot of people say you are a racialist; would you admit in any sense of the word to being a racialist?' Enoch replied in a very smart manner, as he always did: '**First of all I must define it, because if by "being a racialist" you mean "be conscious of differences between men and nations, some of which coincide with differ-**

ences of race" then we're all racialist, I would have thought,
but if by "a racialist" you mean a man who despises a human
being because he belongs to another race, or a man who
believes that one race is inherently superior to another in
civilisation or capability of civilisation, then the answer is
emphatically no.' I do believe that he was not a man who was
full of immense racial hatred. I do not agree with all his words,
especially the words that he expressed in his Birmingham
speech which we all know to be the Rivers of Blood speech.
However, I do agree with him that immigration must be
controlled; there is only so much a nation and most of its
people can handle.

I witnessed something there in India that was very different
indeed; I was witnessing one race segregating itself purely on
caste, so much so that the divisions were beyond belief. In
villages people lived separately, goods were purchased and sold
with allegiance to caste, children were forced to sit on the floor
to make way for higher-caste children in schools, and one was
treated as a pure untouchable regardless of the fact that he or
she might be a teacher or even a lawyer. Most of all I was struck
by the severe loss of dignity that one human can face in
society.

Enoch educated us with his words, and to be honest I saw
his answer to David Frost relating to the question of him being
a racialist as being very open-minded indeed. Enoch gave two
definitions of what a racialist is; I believe that he fell into the
latter category he described to David Frost, and that is to say I
truly believe that he was not a man who considered himself a
superior human to another man or woman simply because of
his race.

I will never forget what my grandfather said to me in
Glasgow when I was eighteen: 'India is not good if you are an
untouchable. Here in Britain, regardless of your social status,
you will still be called "sir" by everyone in the shops and by
officers of the law such as the police, unlike in India where
your humanity is considered so low that "Mr" or "sir" would

be too much for a higher-caste person to call you because of the rules of social apartheid.'

This was a lesson for me, and I took heed of it and really put this into my thought process. All the evidence for this social apartheid was there in front of me; I had been exposed to it earlier when I had been out in India for four months. The sad fact was that I was seeing it in the British Indian community, and that was even worse. I was saddened to see that the very same people that our grandparents knew would never have allowed me or my siblings to have integrated through marriage with them. How sad is it that for a British national of ethnic origin, living in Glasgow in a Western culture, the melting pot of caste discrimination and social apartheid is still simmering? In Enoch's famous words, **'It is like watching a nation busily engaged in heaping up its own its own funeral pyre.'**

At least Enoch was honest about his views. We were meeting people we knew in the temple on Nithsdale Road every Sunday and having a communal meal with them because it was part of our faith and culture to do so. As a youngster, little did I know that the very same people were conscious of their sons and daughters being busily engaged with the lower castes and integrating through having a common interest in football and music, as most teenagers do. I will never forget one girl who came to my school; I met her in the temple and I spoke to her as I generally would because I knew her well and she used to attend the local library. She told me that her mother saw her talking to me and she was told not to speak to a low-caste boy; her mother was petrified that I was going to run off with her daughter. 'Oh, good Lord, the shame of it, just the thought of the suffering that woman must've gone through to see me talking to her daughter!' It was really disheartening to know that she was told off for talking to me about the homework for the Modern Studies class.

In later life in England I could see the higher- and lower-caste illegal immigrant Indians wandering around English towns, desperate to find a wife to get permanent permission to stay in the United Kingdom. Now caste was thrown out of the window. There was no need to implement this social injustice and form of apartheid now; the need to become permanent in this country was so great that anyone would do. English, Scottish, Welsh, Irish or even the dreaded low-caste divorcee, who would have been even more segregated in India for her status: all of a sudden these British women became gold dust for the possibility of permanent residency over here. Shame on the hypocrisy of it all. However, now we are noticing a high increase of Eastern European women being engaged in sham marriages for cash, so the need to chase British women around has been reduced, as EU nationals have the same rights.

There were always higher-caste illegal immigrants in this nation because they had land to sell and this secured their illegal passage to Britain through corrupt means. This applies to Hindus, Sikhs and Muslims equally. I will never forget a recent visit to India where I was in a hairdresser's and I overheard a conversation between the barber and a waiting customer. The customer was very open about his caste and his status in society; he said in a very arrogant manner, 'On my land over here I have over 100 low-caste labourers working for me and I am like a king, but I want to get to Italy or Britain because I want to make more money and that is where all the cash is. The only sad thing is I may have to clean toilets like a low-caste bastard over there in England; oh well, who needs to know? I am still a higher-caste so I am still on top; nothing to lose in terms of status.'

I thought to myself, *I hope the Ukrainians or some other nation pick you up on your way and send you back, you parasite!* I found myself repatriating this guy before he had even left his home nation. Enoch spoke about sending people back in order to prevent civil war in the United Kingdom. I wanted the guy to stay in his own nation and not export his school of thought into my Britain; how dare he disrupt our society? We are a far better people than his way of thinking. The only issue was that I was only flying back into this problem when I returned home; this form of social apartheid had already been success-fully imported into my nation by previous years of immigration.

My grandfather always said that Enoch's words caused him and others of his generation a lot of problems from the people of Glasgow, and other British cities also suffered, as many white British people were up in arms over this issue of immi-gration. However, when one visits a nation one would expect to see the indigenous population; that indigenous population makes the culture, nationality and identity of a nation. Let's face it, the British are known to be very charitable as a nation and we are very well respected for the acts of kindness that British people hand out. If this nation was split between nationalities and the indigenous population were to become a visible minority, what would be left of the British Isles in terms of its attributes? There is no doubt that a different culture being imposed on a race of people can change the law, the way of thinking and the style of living.

My point is that I can enjoy India without the whole of India or Eastern Europe coming to Britain. I am beginning to sound like Enoch now, but I have to be fair to the historical fabric of Britain because that is what has contributed towards its culture and the image it presents to the world. I do accept that my own family came to this nation as early as 1940 and their presence had something to do with the war effort, so, yes, I can accept that their input was due to circumstances at the time. Then again they also gave their freedom to the British Empire, so they left a land of British colonial rule in order to enjoy democracy over here in Britain. So one can see the contrast; however, I do believe that one must be exposed to society and not dominated in order to have an open mind.

When I moved to the south-east of England I could not fathom the lack of knowledge of many British Asians who were born and brought up in this country; some of them were even asking me if Glasgow is in the United Kingdom! I could only blame the policy of **self-segregation** and living in areas that were dominated by Asians. I found it strange that local authorities here were so proud of their perception of a multi-cultural way of life when I could see that a lot of knowledge was not multi-faceted but just horizontal or vertical. Is this a success for Britain, where people segregate themselves to the extent where they know very little about the nation that they now call home?

So yes, I do believe that the behavioural patterns of many people who have come from the Indian subcontinent may have been dictated by the attitudes that are so closely linked to caste discrimination. The one that sticks out the most is 'stay with your own kind, son'; the only issue is that in India they never did accept their own kind of race because of the caste divisions within it. So was Enoch only preaching to the converted? It is a thought that we must elaborate upon because there is no doubt that the first exposure to race and segrega-tion did not come from Enoch's school of thought, which is now known as Powellism, as it is clearly evident that the first inhabitants who came here from the Indian subcontinent were no strangers to being the perpetrators of caste-based social segregation or the victims of this system themselves.

I have a very strong memory of being made to feel like a foreigner, not by some right-wing Scot or Englishman; it was actually by the Indian police and authorities. I was out in India on a three-month visa back in the '80s and I had a return ticket to Glasgow valid for use in four months; this was an issue that needed to be addressed, otherwise it would have been an ideal opportunity for corrupt officials to give me grief at the airport on departure and try to extract money from me. I went to the local police station to let them know that I would like to report myself to them as someone who was going to have to overstay for one month, but to stay on the right side of Indian law I would like to apply for an extension to make it official.

There was an inspector there who looked at me in a very curious manner. 'Where did you get that passport?'

In those days for me the whole world revolved around

Glasgow, so the obvious answer to give was 'Glasgow'. There was no point in telling him that because he did not know where Glasgow was. I said to the inspector, 'It is a British passport and I am British, so I would like a letter from you to give me an extension for one month, please.'

Nobody ever really does say 'thank you' or 'please' out there, so to be honest they just stared at me not knowing what to do. Eventually the mood changed from the inspector. 'There is a fee for this and it is 100 rupees, but if you have pounds I will accept that.'

I had no pounds, but I did have Indian currency. Little did I know that the money was just swallowed up as part of a corruption habit.

'You are a bit late for your extension, little man; did you not know that the British Empire finished back in 1947, yet you come here looking for an extension from me to stay in my country?'

It was hilarious to think that here I was in a place where, had I been seen by a white British national who happened to be over there at the same time as I was, I would have been mistaken for just another Indian. Little would they have known that if they were to witness what was being said to me, they would have noticed that I was just as British as or even more British than them. I was being treated like a foreigner by the officer. 'When did you come to our country?' 'What is your business here?' 'Will you go back as per the date specified on your ticket?' All these questions being thrown at me as a fifteen-year-old kid who really just saw this as a piece of paperwork and nothing else. Eventually he gave me an extension letter. The English was virtually laughable; they could not even spell the name of their own city correctly, let alone Glasgow.

Out of nowhere another officer appeared; they all stood up and saluted him. He looked at me and queried why I was in the station: 'What are you here for? Is there anything we can do for you?' His English sounded really good and he was very capable of holding a good conversation with me.

'Make sure you show the immigration officer that letter,' he said.

I looked at him with an element of respect. 'Yes, I will, but do you want to correct the errors and rewrite the letter? Your officers have not done a very good job, but they did take money from me.'

He smiled at me and took the letter of extension; he made the changes and gave me a sound copy, for which I was grateful at the time. 'Look, make sure you show the immigration officer the letter when he asks for it, OK? If you show him the letter with your passport then those corrupt bastards in Delhi will only say it is the wrong letter. Next time make sure you go to the Indian High Commission in your country and get a six-month visa.'

I was a bit annoyed at this statement, so I made it clear to him that I was allowed only a three-month visa because that was all they were handing out at the time. He still insisted that I must follow the rules because I was a foreigner.

At least Enoch Powell managed to classify the offspring of immigrant children as being citizens of Britain, not ethnically Scots, Welsh, Irish or English but British. I was in a place where I was just known as 'the foreigner' even though I shared the same ethnicity as the very same people whom I classed as my own through a heritage link. In the police station I was a foreigner and back in the village where I stayed I was the low-caste foreigner, so I had two titles, but in my own country I just had one official one and that was Great British. End of!

CHAPTER THREE

Personal Identity and Nationality

Sometimes one will discover that their identity is given to them to suit someone else's status quo or propaganda machine. I will never forget being in college and being asked my national identity by a lecturer who was encouraging debate in the class to boost our communications skills. How could I ever forget this incident? I described myself as British and immediately one student in the class expressed disbelief and dismay: 'Oi, we are Scottish! We have nothing to do with the English flag, OK; have you got that?' What can one say to someone who really does not allow one to employ their democratic right to express their beliefs relating to faith or nationality? I told him that if he felt so strongly about it then he should go to Northgate Passport Office in Glasgow and surrender his British passport with immediate effect. Well, let's face it, I had a good point; this statement soon brought an end to the suppression of my identity by someone who was not willing to do something about an issue that he wanted to dissociate himself from.

I must admit it was a very strange experience because two decades earlier my parents and grandparents were being told by the National Front and uneducated Powellists to 'GO HOME WOGS', so the tables turned when I told this student to establish his identity and find a room within his home that he could call his own, the home being the United Kingdom and the room being a home nation.

Soon after my college experience I started work for the Museums Department in Glasgow and I was very proud to have this opportunity, although certain people I worked with were at times strange to say the least. I loved the Art Gallery and Museum in Kelvingrove because of the surroundings and the beautiful environment; I also had a connection with the place because I was born in the west end of the city, and working in such an iconic place associated with the west end inspired a great feeling of pride in me. My identity and nationality were not an issue to me until one of my closest colleagues admitted to me that when he had heard that a person of Asian origin was going to join the team he had become very apprehensive about the situation. This came to me as a surprise because I was really in a position where I did not see colour but people and colleagues in the same building, so for me the tone of our accents was the distinguishing factor between us. My colleague did admit that once he had got to know me and realised that I was a hard worker and just as much of a Glaswegian as him, he had soon got rid of the apprehension. The only sad factor is that the same apprehension appeared in the hearts and minds of certain people within that office.

This incident reminds me of the time when Enoch Powell would talk about streets being taken over by Commonwealth citizens who were of black or Asian origin and about fear being placed in the hearts and minds of people, namely old women. During the Birmingham speech he said, '**In fifteen or twenty years' time the black man will have the whip hand over the white man.**' Did Enoch Powell contribute towards this way of thinking that I was subjected to? I did not go to the Museums Department to be autocratic or angry with anyone, therefore where did this apprehension come from?

I do believe a lot of it had to do with the very same socialisation process that many Asian people expose themselves to at present and previously underwent when the immigrants came over in significant numbers in the '50s and '60s. When communities feel that they are placed under fear from the unknown, they will huddle together like a football team prior to a match and forge themselves into one community. Even if their own people are terrible and not very nice to know, they will still stick with what they know to be safe rather than risk everything by delving into the unknown. It does cause alienation, there is no doubt about this, and it is inevitable that apprehension will create division amongst people in society. I did ask my colleague if he knew of any Asians when he was growing up, and in his response he used words that were very familiar to me: 'Oh, aye, I knew the darkies in the shop; they were all right to know.' This was obviously a service provider on a commercial scale, so the integration factor was limited. Maybe this is what caused the apprehension amongst certain people within the office; they hadn't interacted with Asians in any other context before. He used the word 'darkies' and to the political correctness brigade he would be classified as a racist. I did not see him as racist; he was just not good with diplomacy skills!

Enoch Powell stated, **'Those whom the gods wish to destroy they first make mad.'** It is strange that when I was being brought up in Glasgow it did not matter what colour you were, whether you were of Asian origin or any other ethnicity, as long as you were faithful to the blue Protestant side or green Catholic side. It is so typical of certain clever politicians to refer to faith and God to make a point and convince the masses. Madness and faith in some cases can be assessed by your allegiance to blue and green. One side will call you intelligent, the other mad.

'As I look ahead I'm filled with foreboding; like the Roman I seem to see the River Tiber foaming with much blood.' These words were linked to power and tragedy; however it is evident that they contained a lot of fear that each inhabitant of every major British city could have had in their hearts and minds because of the influx of the immigrants from the Commonwealth. Each major British city has a famous river and the tragic thought of having the Clyde or the Thames 'foaming with much blood' would undoubtedly place a strong element of fear in the hearts of white communities. Was Enoch right to use such words and use his intelligence to the advantage of his own aims and objectives? In the case of my mother, those words certainly placed her identity and nationality into question amongst the very same people that she thought of as her own city's citizens; others born in this nation suffered the same consequences. It must have been a time of great fear and uncertainty in schools, in places of public gathering and in communities in general.

It was only a couple of decades before this speech that Commonwealth soldiers fought the Germans and the Italians for the freedom of Europe and against the threat of invasion of Britain and the Commonwealth. Those 'wide-grinning' people that Enoch Powell was referring to were perfectly apt and useful for helping the cause to defeat the Nazis but not suitable to live in Britain. On the 9th April 1969 the famous Sikh community leader Mr Sohan Singh Jolly, in the city of Wolverhampton, threatened to kill himself by setting himself on fire because Sikh bus drivers were told they must not wear the turban whilst driving a bus. One surely would have to look at those Sikh Commonwealth soldiers who wore their turbans and went into battle against the German army in occupied lands; that was perfectly acceptable, but any attempt to integrate with those whom the same soldiers fought for was not acceptable. The immigration was not white, so the question one must ask is this: was Enoch's stance based on immigration and numbers only, or could he have convinced the masses only by referring to people of colour because they were different and were perceived to be feared by the white communities of Britain? Was this intelligent politics or just a cheap way to use the colour of skin as the lowest common denominator to win a political point?

Whatever conclusion one reaches, Enoch's approach certainly did cause a lot of British-born Asians to become more alienated and exclude themselves from mainstream society. It is very sad that people who came here to embrace Britain ended up only becoming more loyal to their parents' cultural heritage because it really seemed like the only safe zone to be in, in terms of both physical and mental safety. On the other hand I understand Enoch's sentiment in questioning immigration and numbers; immigration has to be controlled strictly in my view.

Identity became an issue for Asians in Britain. I still meet people today who talk about the time that skinheads would roam around the streets looking for Asians to attack and bully. Sadly the people whom they were targeting came from the same heritage of people who fought for the British against the Japanese and the Germans, so they ended up facing another form of National Socialism on the streets of Wolverhampton and other British towns and cities. However, British tourists were visiting India in their thousands to discover this new hippy trail that was full of love and narcotics, and nobody seemed to attack them on holiday in retaliation for what was happening to British Asians in the UK; they probably did not even care.

More recently I was speaking to a woman who had strong feelings about the white British ex-pats in Zimbabwe, and she made it clear that because they had left Britain and gained prosperity out in Africa, her attitude was 'to hell with them; why should Britain take them back?' What happens to their identities if they are ignored by their own people? Many British Indians in particular have the same issue when they go back to India on holiday; they find that the society over there is not compatible with their way of thinking, even though everyone shares the same ethnicity. It is obvious that the socialisation process has a lot to do with this issue. Recently my father and I went to India on a holiday and I could clearly see how the socialisation process can change a person. My father commented on the driving standards out in India: 'These people do not have the first clue when it comes to driving and health and safety; where on earth are the health and safety rules in this country?' One could only laugh and relate it to the two things that in the minds of many people have contributed to the demise of Britain, and those are too much health and safety and political correctness.

I could not believe our behaviour at times. My father would fall out with relatives and say, 'The people in this place are beyond belief, son!' I suppose he was far more British out there than he was British over here, and that happens to a lot of British Indians when they go there; they become the representatives of the 'Empire striking back'.

In questions of identity, appeasement is always going to be an issue. Many Asians accuse their own people of appeasing the white British in order to get higher up the social hierarchy or to boost employment prospects. This is nothing new; back in the days of the Empire many Indians themselves worked for the British administration in India, and those who were informants were very well rewarded indeed with vast amounts of land. Their own identities changed with this newfound economic prosperity which they had gained by profiting from someone else's misfortune. These people were called 'Gardars', and they were never liked; they were known as backstabbers who cheated their own nation and people. I doubt that these types of characters are out of business over here and out in India where corruption is rife. The fact remains that circumstances can make one change his or her culture just to blend in and be like the rest. This is very evident in London and in the south-east of England where many white youths speak with an accent that reflects what one would hear in the movie *Adulthood*, which is mainly controlled by the Anglicised West Indian accent of London. Asians are no different, modifying their behaviour depending on what social class within Britain they want to be associated with. The socialisation process of an individual can dictate the traits that he or she follows. It is inevitable that an individual or group will be influenced by their socialisation process.

It was only recently that I discovered that it will not be long before the Cockney accent disappears from the streets of London. To me that is a very sad prospect because it is an attribute of London and Cockney rhyme is part of the humour of the city that made it what it is today. I, however, would find it very difficult to lose my accent to any culture or city because I believe that in becoming like someone else you are only insulting yourself. It is a view that will have conflicts and contrasts, but there is no denying that multicultural engagement will have an impact on society. It was meant to bring positive outcomes. However, I truly feel multiculturalism has failed me and I would like to see a uniculture brought into Britain to allow us to celebrate our patriotism and boost cohesion amongst communities.

I have met many white British people who believe that Britain's identity is not patriotic enough. At one time Asians and other ethnic minorities would be fearful of attack or verbal abuse from mainly white people who had racist views as a result of falling for the lies of the National Front and people who shared their ideology. However, now the tables have turned and people are very afraid to say anything in case they get called racist or lose their job for expressing an opinion, whereas at one point patriotism was expressed through verbal and physical anger towards minority groups. Now it seems that the multicultural ethos has ignored the majority to please the minorities of the nation and the onus appears to be on the majority of white people to learn about minority cultures.

It is common to hear these words: 'We've got to learn about all these cultures and religions, mate; don't know why we're not allowed to display the English culture and flag.' There is no doubt that English people feel this way in towns and cities even today, but I do wonder if they themselves for a long time only associated their patriotism with football and other sports. The Scots, meanwhile, have done a very good job in maintaining the Scottish culture and making it user-friendly for ethnic minorities engaging with the mainstream culture of the land. A typical example is the emergence of the groom at Indian weddings wearing the kilt and being led by a bagpiper as he approaches the bride's home. It truly is amazing to link national identity to cultural activities and norms because it can really fuel some positive outcomes. It has resulted in most Asians in Scotland identifying themselves as being Scottish Asian; however, I always identify myself as British of Indian origin.

The British Indians in particular have no real issue with identifying themselves as being British; I have been informed that the majority of Sikhs in this country see themselves as British. This figure would have been much lower soon after Enoch Powell's speech; there is no doubt about that. However, there is still the question of whether Enoch Powell actually ended up doing the nation a favour by promoting Britishness as a positive identity rather than as one to be ashamed of.

Britain still has a long way to go before everyone can feel British, there is no doubt about that. The ice that we are walking on is still very thin; let's face it, when I worked in Fort William as a lecturer I was mistaken on more than one occasion for the new Indian doctor in town. I can never forget the first morning I was travelling to work by bus; the bus driver stopped outside the hospital and shouted, '**There you go, doctor, got you to work on time!**' I thought he was talking to the passenger in front of me, but obviously not because everyone just looked at me. I had to explain that I was a lecturer and not the Indian doctor. It was only at this point that the driver actually apologised about what he had said and assumed.

It goes to show that people can make genuine errors and assumptions that can lead to confusion. The question here is, if I were white, would the bus driver have done the same thing? So surely national identity can be clouded by the colour of your skin, regardless of how British you see yourself as. That day I realised that the bus driver linked my colour with my employment identity and status, yet there was nothing racial about the incident; it was a genuine error. Let's face it, I had a briefcase and a suit on, but now I am engaged within the realms of assumptions; I could have been a car salesman. Who really knows how the mind and identity works? What is evident is that in a small community, particularly a white Scottish community like Fort William, a newcomer is noticed quickly and the colour of a person can make that identification a lot easier. That is not to say that the local community will not be nice to you; it just means that you are part of the society but different. I will never forget how highly the people of the town spoke about a doctor of Indian subcontinent origin; Dr Sen was very highly respected and was always spoken about with high regard. The question is, would he still have been spoken about in the same manner if he were just someone who came to this country and depended on the state and floated around all day doing nothing? Would he have stuck out more based on the colour of his skin?

When I was at school I was taught nothing about the Commonwealth effort during the Second World War. I feel that this would have enabled a lot of children of my age to embrace Britain with a lot more ease; why would one need to feel different if one feels part of a victory? As my life developed I soon realised that the Commonwealth contribution during the war was massive, and it only came to light when a group of Indian World War II veterans visited Glasgow for the Indian 50th Independence celebrations. I was very proud of these old men and the stories that they had to tell us; they were very straightforward people who all wore blue turbans and were very smartly dressed indeed. We took them to George Square and they marched along the square in their uniforms, and the Glaswegian public just stopped and clapped once they found out who they were and the sacrifice that they had made for Britain. I will never forget talking to a fellow Glaswegian who was so emotional that his tears just flooded his eyes; he told me he was born in India and that his father had served with Indian soldiers during the war. He actually told me that he saw Scotland as his second home and that India was his first home as far as his heart was concerned. I would have loved it if he

had met those British Indians who I knew were doubtful about
where they really belonged, because this would have been a
moment where an open mind could develop. We shook hands
and agreed that we must live together in peace, and if that
meant including the Germans then we would accept that as
well as each other.

It was a strange moment for me because all of a sudden I
realised my social education was really developing and sadly
the school that I loved so much had denied me the opportunity to know such a crucial part of my ethnic identity as a
British person. I believe that so much has changed in schools
and colleges where ethnic diversity and respect for others are
important issues in maintaining harmony. In my opinion it is
sad that the onus is on promoting multiculturalism through
dance activities and social events so that the majority of white
people in Britain feel that they must learn about these things
to be less confrontational when dealing with minority groups.
This practice of multiculturalism is really not the answer when
in certain areas there are hardly any white British and more
people from another culture; it is no longer 'multi' for that one
white family who live in a street where they feel as if they are
the minority. Local authorities should be fair when promoting
these sorts of lessons to society because there has to be equilibrium with reality and what is being taught by all of these
diverse activities.

I personally believe that there should be a balance of activities, and I really do honestly support my own statement when
I say I believe that education, local authorities and the political
correctness brigade can make white communities feel guilty
that they are not learning enough about other cultures; sadly
there is little emphasis on minorities learning about the British
culture. I know that has changed now through having to sit a
test to become permanently resident in Britain and therefore
having to learn about Britain's cultures and people, but it is
very late considering ethnic minorities have been here in high
enough numbers since the '50s. If this had been introduced

earlier then more people would have felt some sense of belonging to this nation through the process of learning and that can only be a good thing; sadly it did not happen many years ago. For many, becoming British was a process that one had to follow just to stay safe and secure in Britain; this should have been earned through greater efforts of integration. One side will always blame the other for this, but we must also look at the cultures of certain immigrants into the nation during the '50s and '60s; at this time it was believed that integration could mean the loss of culture, and a lot of immigrant parents were not willing to allow their children to integrate with the white people of this nation for fear of their children losing their culture. It probably was not racial at all, but in the action of preserving culture the ability to identify oneself with Britain was slipping away too far out of reach.

Role models had a lot to do with national identity when I was younger; people who were of my parents' age could identify themselves with the Beatles and other famous people from the '60s. I will never forget my mother telling me that she always felt that John Lennon was the greatest thinker and songwriter within the Beatles. It is just so funny how even she could not fully engage with British culture because her mother was a very old-fashioned woman from the Punjab who was always petrified that her daughter would lose her culture; however, my own mother managed to link a part of her British side to the music of the time and I feel that probably gave her a sense of Britishness to be proud of in her own little way. I could see the hypocrisy of her mother's attitude, and I have some animosity towards my maternal grandparents in that sense. I feel that they lived in a time of perpetual fear that there was no point in fully engaging with the people of Britain because they would be thrown out one day, once Britain managed to get back on its feet again after the war, so they were cautious about integration.

On the other hand I will never forget my mother telling me of a friend who ended up going to Australia for a better life. He

was born in Scotland but was of Indian origin and married a
Scottish woman; she wanted to go to Australia, so he followed
her. It is amazing to think that the world was on the move at
the time; people were travelling from east to west and the Brits
were all going 'down under'. It was all due to economics and I
suppose Britain owed Australia a lot for their contribution to
the war effort, but all they could send them were young
families to boost the nation. There was no way Britain had the
money to send to the Australians as a massive thank-you, so I
suppose they just replaced the people that Australia lost during
the war by providing the country with young families. I am
sure the children of that generation lost their British identity
when they got to Australia, just as many British Asians lost
their Asian identity when they got here, but I am sure that the
strong cultural loyalties and certain fears and prejudices on
both sides slowed the pace of change and acceptance.

In 1982 the Falklands War started and I will never forget
watching it on the evening news. I used to rush back from
school to watch *Newsround* for children and I was just amazed
at what I was watching; for the first time it really hit me hard
that our lads were fighting a very hard battle to win the
Falkland Islands. At my primary school there were kids who
had fathers and older brothers who were in the conflict and
they were really concerned when we started to take losses,
especially when the Argentinians released their deadly Exocet
missiles in our direction. I was really touched by what I was
watching, and the potential shame of losing this conflict was a
worry for me even at a young age because I just could not face
being a British citizen on the losing side. That conflict
contributed towards my British identity and in a way it made
me very concerned about our losses. On the other hand, I was
watching our great military might taking on an enemy located
thousands of miles away and eventually winning.

On my way to school one morning it was just pouring down
in Glasgow and I passed this newsagent's where the news
poster read: 'Argies surrender at Port Stanley – our boys have

done it'. I will never forget walking past that shop, smiling with joy and wondering how the other side felt about losing. I got to school drenched from head to toe; the teachers were all in a happy mood and all the kids who had family out in the conflict had a sense of relief clear on their faces. Although I was still saddened about the losses, I felt very proud of the nation and what it had achieved; the question is, how would my family have felt in the '60s if the conflict had happened then? Enoch made a speech that clearly targeted the immigrant population, and my family felt very bad because their countrymen had contributed towards the victory of World War II and here they were facing prejudices. It is strange to picture how they would have viewed me expressing joy at a British victory considering that people of my ethnicity were being targeted by Enoch and his views. It goes to show that time can change the way people think and behave; I was not a victim of the speech that Enoch made in 1968, so for me uncertainty over national allegiance was not an issue.

Another great moment of British pride came in 2012 when the British Olympic team entered the Olympic stadium to huge applause. I was watching the event at home and the emotion is still hard to describe. The British cyclist Chris Hoy was carrying the Union Jack and leading out the team; for me it was very touching because he is Scottish and from the land of my birth, which made that moment in time a little more special than it already was. Flashbacks to all previous years entered into my mind; events like the miners' strike and the victory in the Falklands just came flooding back and were displayed in the form of tearful emotion. All the successes and tragedies just blended into one and made me feel patriotic like the rest of the nation. We had just pulled through as champions; even though it was just the opening ceremony, I felt that we had already won so much in front of the whole world at the time of that special event in our nation's history. I thought of the moment when my grandparents had told me that they watched the Queen's coronation and how special they felt at witnessing that event in their lifetime; the Olympics made me feel as if I had just joined that club of family members who had embraced historical British moments. I didn't feel different to anyone else; I just felt British, and very proud that our nation were there and were at the epicentre of these games. It felt as if we truly were the champions of the world.

I do wonder how special it would feel if any one of my sons were out there representing our country; the tears would be hard to control. For any British parent this would be a moment to savour with immense pride. It goes to show that, regardless of what we have been through in terms of ethnicity and social economics, we still love our home and nation. We can put our differences to one side, both political and social, and let patriotic emotion take over the heart with a sense of emotive passion that one can only feel if one wants to embrace a national identity.

Tony Benn said that even though Churchill was a Conservative and he was a Labour man, he still supported Prime Minister Churchill in the defence of Britain during the war years. One can look at their ethnicity as much as they want to, but I feel as if the colour of the British passport is all that matters in unifying a nation. If only all felt the same about their communities, county and country.

In the mid-1980s, many Sikh temples opened up their doors to the striking miners and fed them because they were facing a terrible time from Mrs Thatcher's resistance to their demands. This made me play my little role in becoming cohesive with British society; a crisis can bring people together. My mother did the weekly shop as usual, and I have never told her this, but I stole food from our kitchen in the form of tins and I took it to my school; I felt as if I had to do this for the children of the miners who were close to starving in some areas. My school had made a request that we bring in food for the miners and their families, so I was the first who acted upon this and donated some of my mother's shopping list. It made me feel as if I was doing something for my country and its people; I felt very much part of my country, and this small act became a huge boost for my identity as both a Glaswegian and British. I knew that all humans regardless of colour feel hungry and I had to do a little to help.

A few years ago I was driving past a fire station in Northfleet in Kent and I noticed a picket line of firefighters who had an issue with pay; this time the donation came from my own wages, so I did not feel so guilty for helping out. I went home and grabbed a few beers to take to the men and women. My wife did ask what I was doing, so I told her; she smiled and said, 'Only you could feel so strongly about these issues.' I got to the station and handed over the beers. A loud cheer erupted and I got many handshakes from the striking firefighters. Once again this all stemmed from my feeling as if I had a duty to support those very same people who made my country great. I knew this much: that no firefighter would question my ethnicity when it came to saving my life, so what was the issue here? Support the people in our nation at a time of crisis; we Brits are very good at that sort of thing and I am proud of this attribute.

In 1993, soon after I got married, I went off to the local library with my wife because I wanted her to see our great libraries in Glasgow, so it was really a sense of city pride that took me to Langside Library in the south side of the city. I wanted to show her places that meant something to me from my childhood. I was totally amazed to learn that MK Gandhi got a medal for his services during the Boer War; I learned this from an old man in the library who used to talk to me about British war history. I could not understand how a man who opposed British rule in his nation managed to get a medal from his rulers. He set up an ambulance service for the British war injured out in South Africa and for that he was awarded a medal. That information really made me think about humanity and nationality; both humanity and nationality can be the components of a good citizen in an appropriate context.

I had to watch the movie *Gandhi* to find out more and I was amazed by the scene where he was in South Africa giving a talk about the cruel pass laws that were being introduced. Once he had given the speech he sang the British national anthem, and that was something that really made me think about loyalty and allegiance. Regardless of how a group of people treat each other, there is no anger towards the soil of the land. Maybe that revelation gave me an open mind to analyse the behaviour that relates to identity and nationality.

Winston Churchill once said, '**India is a geographical term. It is no more a united nation than the Equator.**' Unity is imperative; it supports national identity. If a nation is not united, how can it stand against an aggressor who wants to take it over? What was Winston really saying here? It truly is a deep statement. If one does not feel united, then it is fair to state that walking in a circle wondering about a sense of belonging will only make dizziness develop into confusion. It is essential for me that all British nationals regardless of ethnicity unite so that we may never need to hear Churchill's words from a foreign president or prime minister relating to the United Kingdom. It would be a sad day for our nation if that became what was thought of us, considering we have truly achieved so much over the years.

On the 13th April 1919 a terrible massacre occurred in the Indian city of Amritsar; it was a horrific act by General Dyer, who instructed his troops to open fire on a crowd of men, women and children who were having a public meeting. This incident still is very much in the hearts of all people who are Indian and British Indian. One may ask why I should be proud of my Britishness when such a terrible atrocity was committed by this one disgraced British general. I have to emphasise that this incident changed a lot of relations with the British in India; it certainly added more fuel to the independence struggle for Gandhi and his followers. It is really sad to think that between the war years of 1914 and 1918 so many Indian soldiers gave their lives for the British in the bloody theatre of war and this was the thanks they got for it. I still feel very ashamed of this incident.

I will never forget visiting the garden where this atrocity was committed by this mindless general; in 2008 I embarked upon the very same footsteps that General Dyer took to conduct this horrendous massacre, to see for myself how it must have felt for the victims of this tragedy. I came across a group of white British youngsters who were on a tour of India and they were really ashamed of this tragedy; it was clearly evident from the look on their faces that they were disturbed to see the well that people jumped in to escape being killed by a British bullet. It was by accident that we started to talk to each other, and my Glaswegian accent was the biggest factor that determined the move to make discussion. My father and my uncle were explaining to me what had happened so long ago and how it had impacted the independence struggle. The youngsters were from England and they heard my Glaswegian accent whilst my dad and I were engaged in historical issues; all around them were brown faces, including mine, so they were shocked but pleased to come across this pleasant surprise. One lad asked the critical question, 'Rangers or Celtic, mate?' I was amazed at this and the laughter just spilled out from both sides.

They were so happy to see someone from back home and they asked me what my perspective was on the whole situation, considering I am British of Indian origin. I was really happy that they engaged with me because I am sure that it was an education for them to find out what my feelings about this tragedy were. I told them that I felt really saddened about this part of British history, but that these were not the actions of a nation but of an individual who sadly shamed an entire nation. They were intrigued by my open-minded nature, but I made it clear that I was just as ashamed as they were because I am British and it does hurt to know that through my nationality I am associated with this issue.

A young girl asked me a question once she had cleared her

tears up with the tissues that I gave her: 'How would you relate this incident to any other bad memory of British rule?'

It took me a while to respond to her and she stared at me, thinking I was going to give a response that would have caused more embarrassment. I took their minds to Northern Ireland and told them in a very assertive manner, 'In 1972, Bloody Sunday was Derry's Amritsar for the victims of that tragic day.' They were taken by surprise by my answer, but it was the only one I could give them and it managed to establish a balance between tragedy in India and the one in Northern Ireland.

It was very emotional to meet other British people like me out in such an iconic place that meant so much to my family and many other Indians. It was also a moment for me to reflect on identity. When I looked at my passport, I realised that I was not a national of India but someone who was linked to the nation through heritage. My uncle, a former Indian Army officer, actually put a stamp on the envelope of this issue; he asked why on earth, if I was regarded as an Indian by the Indian government, I needed a visa to go there. We both looked at each other and I pointed out that he too requires a visa to visit Britain. His response was very thought-provoking: 'Yes, son, but I have no blood link to your country whereas you have a blood link to India, so it is fairer for your government to require a visa from me, but I think we are being unfair to you. Then again, I suppose we are right to treat you like this; you may end up staying here for 150 years again. We would not welcome the Empire back again, would we now?'

In this way my British identity was confirmed by my own family and I had to agree with them because I was so different to them in so many ways; my socialisation process in my nation of Britain had already confirmed that.

I wonder what Enoch Powell thought of this incident in Amritsar, because he had a close relationship with India; he actually served in Delhi as a brigadier in the British Indian Army. I do question the perception that people had of this man. He gave a speech in Parliament on the Mau Mau

Rebellion Hola Camp massacre in Kenya by the British troops who killed eleven rebels in a non-combat situation. It was really evident through his words that he was disgusted by the way in which this whole situation ended. He clearly condemned his parliamentary colleagues for calling the Kenyans 'sub-human'; he demanded equal treatment for enemy combatants. To me it shows a different side to this man. Did his Christian values have a role to play in his condemnation of this atrocity? The point I am making here is that we have a man who was always branded as a racist, yet he actually could not agree with the way in which these Africans were treated. Why did he make this speech? What was the motive behind it? Was it moral conviction relating to his faith? Whatever his reasons, he gave one of his finest speeches relating to this issue of inhumane treatment.

Enoch was also against the American invasion of Vietnam; he commented on the conflict by saying, 'The point is that the Americans do not live in South-East Asia, whereas the North Vietnamese and their neighbours do.' I do wonder if he had the same opinion of the British taking over India and making it the 'jewel in the crown' of the British Empire. Was this a case of the pot calling the kettle black or was he genuine in his statement relating to Vietnam? How well did the British public really know this man? At times he would show a very considerate side to his way of thinking, and he also showed a very non-negotiable side to his views.

My own personal identity is noticed every day here in England. There has never been a social event where I have not been reminded that I am Indian with a Glaswegian accent. This is something that I find to be funny and also concerning; Britain has many cities and accents, so why should I be identified as being so different? In the south-east of England I personally have noticed that there is a massive expectation that all people of Indian or any other ethnic origin must only speak with the mother tongue accent or one of the accents surrounding the M25: London, Kentish etc. I always remind the people who make these comments that if I took a person of black or Asian origin with an English accent to Scotland, they would hear comments on their accent themselves; I then get told that it is so racial of the Scots to do this to our people! It truly comes down to lack of knowledge relating to other British cities and the inhabitants of those places; one would expect to find an Indian restaurant in any British city, but if the person who is serving at the restaurant speaks with an accent from elsewhere in the UK it all of a sudden becomes something to mock or look at in surprise. Surely the children of the first immigrants of the '50s and '60s would speak with the accent that they were exposed to every day.

This can come down to the wider stereotypical notion of what a Scottish, English, Welsh or Irish person is supposed to look like, and the question of what exactly it is that makes someone uniquely different to another person from a different part of the British Isles. It is evident that people can feel comfortable with ethnic minorities if they act and behave like the mainstream population, and what could be closer to home than shared traits such as accent and culture? However, I am different, so I get noticed more. If my accent were south-eastern English my ethnicity would not even be noticed, would it now?

A lot of my white friends have been embarrassed when the question of my accent has arisen during social events, and they are amazed by my patience. I have to be patient; I am under the spotlight, and I have to portray an image of Glasgow that is civil and decent, so why should I lose my patience over such a question? I have had other people ask me if the Scots treated me well back in Glasgow based on my colour, and this question has always raised an eyebrow because it was not us back in Scotland who had race riots; that all happened here in England. Of course I faced challenges in Scotland; when one left the city of Glasgow it would be very rare to see an ethnic minority person wandering around another city or town. Then again, this had no impact on my early and teenage socialisation process because when you are exposed to your environment you do become part of it and take on some of its characteristics. I always knew that in England there were issues with race and riots, but this never caused me any issues because we had minorities that were small in number, therefore it is evident that Scotland and other parts of Britain did not attract so many immigrants as England managed to. It is obvious that the industries were all in England; in the late 1960s the industries of Scotland were dying and those of the midlands were growing due to the ease of transportation of manufactured goods, so that area would attract more immigration than Scotland ever would.

The statement I made about minorities being small in number relates to what Enoch discussed during the David Frost interview; he spoke about the ease of getting on with minority groups if they are small in number. Numbers seemed to be the issue that he focused on, and it is obvious that I agree with him on the issue of numbers. How would the people of India feel if the whole of China walked into their land and established their culture and language in villages, towns and cities? Would they accept it? There is no way on God's Green Earth they would accept it. It is fair to ask the question of whether Enoch was right to discuss numbers in towns like Southall and Wolverhampton.

Enoch spoke about practicality and limiting numbers. When I lived in Glasgow I would hear how people would not want to move into an area like Pollokshields because it had a high ethnic minority population who were mainly of Pakistani origin. I will never forget being in a pub in Glasgow where I engaged in a discussion with a group of Asian youths who were of Indian and Pakistani origin; they dreaded the prospect of having to live in Pollokshields because they did not want to be associated with the stereotype of the area. How times have changed since Enoch's days in Wolverhampton and in many parts of London where so many English people did not want to live near a black or Asian family; now I have noticed how far certain ethnic minorities want to be from each other. I must say I can relate this to the more embedded generations of ethnic minorities who do not need to live in an area dominated by Asian people just so that they feel safe, with cultural and linguistic needs catered for. Since the 1960s that has all changed because of the socialisation and cohesion that the newer generations have engaged in, having been born and brought up in this nation.

All this makes one ask the question of whether the upbringing of certain Asian youths makes them forget an element of their identity; it is certainly the case in some areas that in order to fit into mainstream society certain Asian youths feel it is more appropriate to turn against their ethnic culture. A lot of them still cannot speak their mother tongue but can understand what is being said. God help them if they ever go to India for a holiday; they would not have a leg to stand on if they had to barter for goods in shops. I am bilingual and very proud of that, but one must not get embroiled between cultural allegiances and national identity; just eating Indian food and watching Bollywood on a daily basis does not make one Indian, that is for sure. However, there are so many kids over here who believe that what they see in Bollywood movies is a true reflection of Indian society. That, I can assure you, is far from reality, but then again that is all many really have at their disposal to stay in touch with their ethnicity and identity.

CHAPTER FOUR

Hindrances to Social Interaction

Enoch was not wrong when he spoke about cultural differences. There is no doubt that British culture, from imperial measurements to food, is totally different to that of the rest of Europe. Great Britain is an island and it has its own insular identity; no wonder it is different.

As for integration of cultures, I do believe Enoch was influenced by the fear of violence and trouble erupting on the streets of Britain; there is no doubt he was influenced by the race riots in America just after the death of Martin Luther King.

The fear of ghettos was probably in his mind, and the emergence of a new problem on the streets of Britain. Racial profiling could have developed; even if certain groups of immigrants made an effort to integrate there would overall have still been a problem as he saw it. The riots over in America happened just a little over two weeks before his famous speech in Birmingham. Enoch was out in India, specifically Delhi, and it is obvious that he liked the nation very much; he even learned Hindi and Urdu, as he saw himself as a likely candidate for the great position of Viceroy. **It has been reported that he would speak to his Asian constituents in Wolverhampton in the Urdu and Hindi languages.** It is not easy to speak these languages, let alone to try to integrate with the communities at the same time. There is no doubt he believed that integration was necessary in order to learn the language; how else could one learn the language in those days?

I am sure Enoch was also aware of another issue that still

haunts many people in India, Pakistan and Britain. In 1947 Britain had to partition India into two nations, India and Pakistan; the western part became Pakistan, and this affected mainly the state of Punjab. Nobody knew where the line would be drawn between the two nations, and this caused mass murder and genocide on both sides. The atrocities are too sickening to even write for me because my father's family were caught up in the hell that visited earth in 1947. People still blame the British for the partition of India, but this is not really right in my opinion because the Muslim League at the time were petrified that they would have been persecuted anyway by the new independent Indian government. India had to be split into two because there was no way that Hindus, Sikhs and Muslims could get on. This was not the fault of the British because before they even ruled India atrocities had already taken place. When the Moguls invaded India they raped, killed and tortured the Hindus and Sikhs, so the fire was already burning with memories of the sacrifices that were made. With the British in control there was still law and order; if they had left far too early without reaching a compromise, one can just imagine what could have happened with corrupt politicians and evil people who only wanted to use religion to pursue their own aims.

In 1947 entire villages were wiped out and women on both sides became sexual slaves and converted to Sikhism, Hinduism and Islam. Trains were used to transport people from the new nations of India and Pakistan. The killing was disgusting on both sides. I know about this because my own family became refugees in their own country and had to travel to a safe haven, where they shared their ethnicity with the folk of the land, just to stay alive. The same applied to Muslims who had to leave cities like Delhi, Hoshiarpur and Amritsar. I will never forget talking to a woman named Theresa who sat next to me on a flight from Amritsar to London and told me of the horrors that she had witnessed. She told me that she was spared rape and death because she was a Christian; she told me she had walked past a group of Muslim men who were taking the jewellery off woman they had raped and killed. As for the Sikhs, she told me that she had watched them kill people with swords in an open street, butchering everyone in sight apart from Hindus and Christians. It must have been sickening to know that innocents on both sides suffered so much whilst evil people on both sides were prospering. My grandfather was right; **the only people that profit during troubles are thieves and killers, and all the rest just suffer.**

What was Enoch thinking of when he made that Rivers of Blood speech? Was the famous Ancient Roman poet Virgil the only influence in his mind? Surely in his mind he must have been aware of the civil unrest in India during partition; he must have thought about the way that the people of India and Pakistan treated each other during that terrible time. What was he more concerned about: the Indians and Pakistanis rioting with each other or turning against the white population?

Enoch was a Christian, so just how did he view the religions of India and Pakistan? This is a serious question. If all the immigrants coming over were Christian, where would his morality have stood then: knee-high in the River of Blood or just accepting of the fact that they were just as Christian as him? In my own thoughts and opinions, I doubt his stance would have been swayed; I am sure he would have called for control, and rightly so. Let's face it, we would not be comfortable if huge numbers of French people just crossed the Channel and started to live here; regardless of their colour and faith, there still would be objections. I am sure of this.

Many questions arise when one thinks of Enoch's perception of ethnic minorities; however, there is one issue for sure, and that is the fact that he was certainly not in favour of any type of immigration that was not controlled or monitored with caution. The world had not long come out of terrible atrocities with the Holocaust in Europe and the butchery at the Punjabi border between India and Pakistan. All of these events really shaped the world and the way people thought about each other, so what made Enoch any different? Certainly he was not going to appease or ignore government policy with his vision and linguistic ability; he was going to make a rather strong comment on the issue of immigration that was certainly brewing in society. Not many people will agree with me, but did he manage to avoid civil unrest by making the government realise that they had to control immigration from the Indian subcontinent? One only has to look at the way in which Indian and Pakistani communities separated them-selves from each other when they got to Britain; Bradford has a strong Muslim community and Wolverhampton has a strong Indian community. I believe that because the partition and its dreadful atrocities were still fresh in the minds of people, creating geographical divisions in Britain was the only way that they could live in harmony. The mindsets of both communities were economic, so harming each other was not on the agenda, but at the backs of their minds there probably was a lot of mistrust due to what had happened in 1947.

Winston Churchill once said, 'The English never draw a line without blurring it.' Sadly the line that was created between India and Pakistan was blurred out with blood that completely obscured the vision of humanity.

My father always said that the trains transporting goods to the seaports during the British Raj in India were always well protected, but somehow the British administration left the Hindus, Sikhs and Muslims to kill themselves on the trains of blood. He did admit that it was not the fault of the British that these people could not live together, but the British just packed up and left them to it after taking all the economic benefits out of the nation. A valid point indeed, but the killing was not ordered by the British; this was done by Hindus, Sikhs and Muslims themselves, who were fighting for land village by village. One has to remember India was really backward in 1947; there was no law and order, and there were no emergency services that could respond to a call for help. Nobody knew where the line of partition would start or end, so capturing land by killing the innocents on both sides would determine whether it would be a Muslim or Hindu majority India. This was the bloody mindset of the people at the time of partition.

Bob Marley once said, 'You never know how strong you are until being strong is your only choice.' My family had to be strong to face the horrors of partition and then to face the challenges of Britain, so for them the Enoch speech in favour of controlling immigration may have been right in principle but the words used by him were questionable. The words that he used were certainly in my opinion bordering on creating an atmosphere that could erupt into civil unrest, but the question is, did he want to gain political stature by instilling fear into the hearts of white British people? When an MP claims that he has received a letter from an anonymous source we can all normally tell who that anonymous source is. I still believe that people did approach him in Wolverhampton or he himself went out on a fact-finding mission; there is no doubt that the numbers were visible and so was the frustration for Enoch and the public.

Integration is still an issue that I feel can be improved upon by all communities. In the early days of immigration it was the men who could speak English with greater ease because the majority of women stayed at home with the kids; for those women, life was really just confined to the home and other women of the same origin who stayed at home. They were the real losers when it came to integration. A lot of Asian men did not like their women going to work, but I am not being biased here. In particular Indian men were probably more lenient with regard to their women leaving the home to go to work; this was not widespread, but was still more common than in other communities from the Indian subcontinent.

Integration was always going to be an issue because language was a barrier and so was faith; the only place that people of Indian origin could really meet was in the temple on a Sunday, and that was where most of their social integration took place. It is sad that that was all they really had because of the barriers that were placed by the fear of integration, and this fear created a huge gap in race relations for a very long time. Then again, some had good reason for being in fear of gangs, racial abuse, police harassment and being made to feel the odd one out because of the way they dressed or spoke. It was never going to be easy for them, in the same way that it would not be easy for me now to go to live in an Eastern European nation like Poland, where I would be subjected to severe racial abuse from certain football hooligans who are very well known for being involved in extreme right-wing activities. I would not lock myself in some Polish closet, but I would stand tall as a British national and make it clear that I would never go to a place where I was not going to be made to feel welcome. Then again, I do have a choice that I exercise well; others were not so fortunate at the time of immigration in the '50s and '60s.

Although I mention that some had a hard time, I would like to add that there are many people whom I know in Wolverhampton who had a fantastic time in settling into the city and meeting certain English people who were just brilliant to the newcomers into the nation. One needs to remember that a lot of the indigenous British kids whom the immigrant kids met had grandparents who were born in India or who served out there for the British Raj, so there was an affiliation with India for some British people. There was one such woman named Stella Reekie from Glasgow; she did a lot for the immigrants who came into the city and she is very well remembered as a human being of great understanding. I have been told that she spent many hours talking to my paternal grandfather; being a teacher he must have had a lot of questions for this great woman of humility and understanding. I wish I too had known her, because people like her only come to a city once in a lifetime. Mr Saggu, a well-known and respected Indian man who lived in Glasgow, spoke at a celebration of her life and he referred to Psalm 139, especially focusing on the words:

Such knowledge is too wonderful for me,
Too high to grasp, too great to understand.

In Mr Saggu's words: 'Stella Reekie was too great for me, too high to grasp and too great to understand ... She suffered for us to her last breath, so that we ... could get together, enjoy ourselves together, and learn to live in love, peace and harmony.'

What is truly amazing about this woman is that she came from near Gravesend and ended up in Glasgow as a result of circumstances. In 1998 I moved to Kent from Glasgow and established Kent as my home, and it is a place that I have grown to love very much indeed. Stella Reekie was a nurse at the Belsen concentration camp, so she saw the horrors and the devastating effects, both psychological and physical, that hatred can bring to communities. Stella worked in Pakistan and learned Urdu whilst she was out there helping people. She returned to Glasgow as a community worker, helping the new immigrants from the Indian subcontinent to get help in medical and other social issues that needed addressing. She used her linguistic skills to help these new immigrants settle into the city of Glasgow. I have heard from my mother that she left no stone unturned in helping these people make Scotland their new home; they responded well to this offer of help and they benefited by integrating with the people of the city because of this great woman.

The contrast between people like Enoch and Stella is very strange; here we have two people who both were exposed to the language of the Indian subcontinent and visited the place. One left a famous legacy, and the other is not so well known throughout Britain for her efforts to promote good-natured and kind-hearted Britishness in a caring and loving manner to the people who suffered at the hands of the Nazis. On the other hand Enoch himself was a strong Christian who would certainly have respected Stella Reekie, and here am I as a British national, trapped between both of them as I write about them. I have to be fair in showing consideration, but Stella did touch my family in a personal way and I believe that she certainly did England proud by going to Scotland and showing the people how beautiful an English rose can really be when it touches someone's heart. Our differences make us unique, and no doubt Enoch was unique. In the case of these two figures, one Brit was an expert in exercising the mind and raising questions; the other Brit provided healing and care. I am attached to both through nationality; however, we must look at the dichotomy of these two people, especially from Stella's angle. She ended up having to help the new Commonwealth immigrants not just in a medical sense but in a social context, as a result of the words that Enoch used. The attitudes and perceptions created by the Rivers of Blood speech probably caused her more grief and hindrance as she went around the city of Glasgow trying to ascertain help for people.

I am very proud of Stella Reekie, and I hope the people of Glasgow, especially the British Asians who were born in Glasgow, never forget what this one Great British citizen did for their parents and grandparents.

Integration with other British Asians was not an option for people like Indian doctors who were placed in rural communities, because most Asian communities were only based in industrialised towns for employment reasons. For these people, integration with the community in which they lived was an experience that they had to get to grips with; then again, a lot of them were very well respected because they were seen as very well-educated people and there was a need to keep them happy in the community at all costs. I do not believe that the rural white communities were nice to the doctors solely because they were in need of them; I honestly believe that they viewed them with a lot of respect, and that is something that is regarded with thanks by a lot of the Indian doctors and their families.

However, many of those who worked in manual jobs were

seen as people who were taking over jobs and bringing into Britain a new culture that was not welcomed in a lot of cases. It must have been hard to work in a place where even at tea break time there was segregation. In the Kelvingrove Art Gallery and Museum there are photographs on display that show the early Indian and Pakistani settlers in the city of Glasgow; there is a picture of bus drivers having a break and the two Asian drivers are sitting on a table on their own in the canteen, having their tea. Was this due to workplace apartheid? It could have been that it was the only chance for them to exercise their mother tongue during the working day.

I do remember that when my uncle became a bus driver in Glasgow he told us about the arguments that broke out in the depot over Asians taking over jobs. I remember saying to a friend in college that the jobs had to be taken over because Britain had already sent thousands of people to Australia on a £10 ticket. He soon agreed that this was a fact and that it was wrong of the government not to highlight this to the British public and make them realise that the Commonwealth's people had to be shifted around to make the Commonwealth work. I must say that there was no factor of immense wealth amongst common men and women in the '60s and '70s; it was just a struggle to get by.

Asian communities also have to take part of the blame for lack of integration; they did not disperse themselves around towns and cities very well. They stayed in certain areas and before long they would invite others of the same ethnicity to come and stay close to them in the same street. This soon drove a lot of the white people out of the area because they began to feel unsafe with the unknown, and I can understand the fear that they probably had. It is sad that the economic prosperity relating to house prices tumbled down in those areas as a result of the stereotypes that were applied to the areas where lots of Asians lived.

I came across a woman in Swanley to whom I was teaching literacy and she made it clear that she left London to get away from all the blacks in the area that she lived in. I asked why she felt threatened and she said that she did not want her daughter being married to a black man. She was clear about this and she felt that it would have been a source of shame for her to have mixed-race grandchildren. I could not understand her mind-set because she always spoke about giving money to poor African countries to support children who were suffering from war and drought. It really did come as a surprise to me when she told me that she herself was the child of Irish immigrants! It just goes to show that the longer-established immigrant somehow becomes more significant on the hierarchy of immigration status and social deprivation.

Integration for the Asians was also an issue in the early days for those who had daughters; a lot of the Indian and Pakistani people just could not bear the prospect of their daughter getting married to a white man because of the cultural differences and religious differences. Many mixed marriages did take place, but a lot of these couples were shunned by both communities and difficulties were faced by the offspring of these relationships. Mixed marriages are still looked upon with uncertainty even today, but it is a lot easier than in the '60s, '70s and '80s, that is for sure. They are more clearly visible on the streets of England than in Scotland because of the higher numbers of immigrants who settled in the southern parts of Britain. The majority of mixed marriages involving people from the Asian community are still frowned upon by that community and a lot of this has to do with faith and cultural issues, whereas in England in particular mixed relationships between white and black seem to be more acceptable regardless of the fact that in many cases the female is white. Mixed marriages where one half is an Asian woman are really looked upon with distaste by the majority of the Asian communities in Britain. However, I have noticed over the years that if the male is Asian and his partner is white then it is not so frowned upon.

Language was clearly the problem in a lot of cases. I still feel uneasy when Indian people speak Punjabi in front of white British people. It is in my opinion not only rude but also very inappropriate for a community to do this, especially when they can speak English really well. What need is there for this when we can speak whatever language we want in the comfort of our own homes? In public, it should only be English that is spoken. If someone says that I am wrong then that is a reflection of the same ethos that causes the problem to continue today; how on earth can someone complain about people pulling them up for this when the language of this land is English? English has to be spoken in this land, in my opinion, because the people who do not speak the language are the very same ones who are costing local services through translation services and are delaying their own better employment prospects. I can understand if someone has just got to the country – we need to help those people to integrate by helping them with the language; this would have benefits for all, both social and economic – but I am referring to people who have been here for over forty years and still cannot call themselves literate in spoken or written English.

One may turn around and say that I am wrong in making this statement because the Welsh themselves speak their language openly in public places. I have to disagree with anyone who brings this issue up; they have to ask themselves the question, is Wales not part of the United Kingdom? Cornish is also a language rooted in the UK. Nobody has the right to criticise or question the languages of this land that were well established before any immigrant came to this nation.

I have to defend this issue because proficiency in language helps one to integrate into society in a better and wider context. I accept that people do not like being told to speak English, but if one makes Britain their home and gains from the prosperity this land has to offer then they must respect it by speaking the language in public. People will always love their mother tongue and I do not disagree with this, but compatibility and adaptability are required for integration to become a success. Even if that success is small, it is still a stepping stone towards more integration if we can communicate with each other and thus open more integration opportunities. With the huge increase of Eastern Europeans in our nation, I am now seeing a lot of Asian people complaining that they cannot understand what is being said and find it rude; the tables seem to have turned! I always add salt to the question by saying, 'Hurts, does it not, when you are left out of the conversation?' Now we know how our indigenous fellow countrymen and women felt.

On a visit to India I spoke English to my wife on the phone and I was prompted no fewer than ten times to speak Punjabi by my cousins, who really felt alienated and insecure. I asked them how an English person would feel if they spoke Punjabi over in Britain in a public place, and their attitude changed rapidly. They felt that it would not be an issue because they do not speak English, so it would have to be permitted. I then asked what the situation would be like for them if they lived in Britain and could speak English but chose not to. My cousins felt that they could speak English at work and in public places but would certainly return to their mother tongue at home to keep it fair. At least I got them to face a scenario where they felt as if they were being alienated by a relative who could have spoken in Punjabi to his wife but chose not to. It was a good social experiment because it certainly made me realise how an indigenous British person feels when he or she is faced with this situation on a daily basis in Britain.

I still walk into pubs and I hear certain languages being spoken very loudly indeed. I was once in a pub along with a group of men who were not born in this nation but were immigrants from India, and there was one Englishman in the pub who felt very uncomfortable sitting there having to hear this alien language. I asked the men to speak English considering that they were in a public house and they made it clear that they did not want to. Now in my opinion that is ignorance. What annoyed me was that they were talking about football and the last time I checked most Englishmen could talk for hours relating to football; they obviously denied themselves the chance of integration.

They had to ask me a question about how to get to White Hart Lane; coming from Glasgow, how the hell did I know? I asked the Englishman and he was overjoyed that someone was actually engaging with him because he had endured this conversation that he could not be part of for hours. When I approached him to ask him where White Hart Lane was, he responded by saying, 'Hey, glad to meet you, mate; my mum is from Glasgow and all of my uncles are Celtic supporters.' Before you knew it we were in full swing, conversing about our respective football teams and cities. It just goes to show how powerful language can be in striking up a friendship or eliminating loneliness.

The other men who were speaking Punjabi asked me where I had learned English because they thought I had been born and brought up in India. I responded after a minute because I wanted to capture their silence and attention; non-verbal communication can be one strong technique to catch attention. 'I learned it here in Britain; I was born here and I am British of Indian origin.'

They accepted this and then they asked me, 'Where did you learn to speak Punjabi and Hindi?'

I told them in a very sarcastic manner, 'Oh, I made the effort to learn it and it was not that sore, you know.'

They knew what I meant and then they called the English-man over to talk to him about Tottenham and the forth-coming match. It had taken a Glaswegian to sort out the linguistic barriers that had caused alienation for that poor Englishman.

I was actually proud of the fact that I did not see colour; I just saw people. I soon realised that there was still an issue with cultural integration, although the local authorities and government always say that there is no problem. Try and tell that to the Englishman who could not understand a word being spoken; all he wanted to do was integrate with people, but those men used a weapon of alienation, and that was the tongue. The tongue can heal, but it can also pierce through someone. I felt sorry for the guy because at the end of the day he could have told them off and instructed them to speak English, but he did not because he was probably scared of the fact that he was outnumbered. When I walked in he felt at ease because I had my Celtic top on and he knew that it was a club that he could relate to.

This incident really made me feel that there was something still wrong with integration in British society. To be frank, I really believe that the English in particular, unlike the Scots or Welsh, are too cautious of being called racist; a nation cannot function with this fear factor.

This is something that has to be said, in my view. If someone feels that it is prejudiced, then that is their prerogative, but I do believe that the people of Britain can really get on with other cultures if the linguistic issue is sorted out, especially in public places. A lot of Asian people whom I know always say to me that when they are in the pub nobody talks to them; I always tell them this is due to the fact that nobody can understand them. It is not their colour that is the issue; it is their linguistic barrier that is preventing anybody else from entering the discussion. I am sure that many people will agree with this statement because it is so true that people who segregate themselves tend to blame others for not engaging with them, and in my view it is very unfair for them to reach this conclusion.

I do ask myself a question from time to time, and that is about my own socialisation process in Scotland. Is it the fact that we are not so restricted back home and not so scared of the 'racist' label that has permitted positive discussion to take place? Since moving to England from Scotland I have felt sorry for some people, in Kent in particular, when they have approached me and said, 'Hey, mate, not being racist but where does your accent come from? Don't mean to be racist, mate, but is it from Scotland or Ireland?' For heaven's sake, they are petrified of being called prejudiced or racist when an accent is not restricted by race but more of a location issue and anyone who is exposed to it for long enough will pick it up. It is sad that it has got to this stage, and I tell these people not to be so scared about asking the question that they want to ask me.

I would love to find the people who have placed this fear in the British people, and in fact more so in the English people, because this really is causing a hindrance. We cannot have open debate or informal discussion where one party is terrified of losing their job by the morning because they might have the label of 'racist' placed on them for asking a simple enough question. This does infuriate me at times because it makes perfectly decent people look as if they are talking to a communist spy who may have them sent to some work camp in North Korea. These sorts of perceptions have hindered integration because many English people are too scared to say something just in case it is all taken the wrong way and someone gets barred from a pub or disciplined at work. It is just a hindrance that has been caused by those who surrender too quickly in the process of appeasing others for the sake of it. These are my opinions; others may hold different views. I believe in British democracy, so they are more than welcome to write a book relating to their views, but I do want to defend the democratic rights of all British nationals regardless of cultural or colour differences.

A major barrier to integration comes from the Indian subcontinent communities themselves. I will never forget one occasion in Ealing, where there are a lot of Indian Gujarati people. I found myself in a supermarket on a normal Saturday afternoon. Two female members of staff who were of Indian Gujarati origin just kept speaking Gujarati in front of the customers; I really found this inappropriate because we were not in India but in West London and it just isn't fair to do this in front of customers. One of the Englishmen had had enough of this and asked them how they had got their jobs if they could not speak English; they responded in a very smiling manner and told him that they did not feel as if they were doing something wrong, but they did apologise to him.

I approached the members of staff and asked them where I could find Worcestershire Sauce for a meal that I was preparing for a long cycle journey, and they spoke to me in Gujarati again. Now, I am aware of the fact that India has a lot of local state languages, but I only know two: the national language, which is Hindi, and Punjabi, which is the state language where my grandparents came from. I could not believe it, so I asked them if they felt that I would not feel offended because I was of the same ethnic origin.

One of the girls replied in a manner of concern and curiosity, 'Oh, it is the manner in which you speak English, sir. I was under the impression you came from India with your accent, but I am not too sure.'

I was amazed by this girl's inability to identify accents. With my eyes wide open, I asked her, 'Do you not know where Glasgow is, and honestly are you not aware at all that this place is nowhere to be found in India?'

At this point she looked at me with her chest puffed out like a soldier standing at attention, ready to respond to a visiting dignitary, 'Oh yes, I know a lot of Eastern Europeans have come to London, so let me guess now, sir. Let's call it Latvia.'

I burst out laughing at this point because I had really had enough of this social spectacle. I just had to ask her if she knew where Scotland was. She replied in a very flirtatious manner, 'Oh yes, sir, the land of kilts; I know about this place because I stack their whisky on the shelves.'

I thought to myself that even if there are a minority who have terrible geography and little ability to identify accents, it still should be within the basic education of kids in this nation to identify their own British cities, but it comes down to whether someone takes an interest in their own nation. One can also blame this incident on the self-segregation in certain areas in Britain, where certain communities just lock themselves away and stay amongst their own kind; in these cases it is obvious that they will prove to have minimal knowledge of the wider geographical landscape of Britain and its peoples. I am not saying that in Scotland the people are experts in British geography, but overall they can identify an Englishman in verbal discourse through accent and dialect.

It still amazes so many white British people when I speak to them about their county or local culture; they seem to be surprised that a man of Indian origin can relate to their local culture by sharing knowledge. I always ask why one British citizen should be surprised by another's knowledge when that other comes from the same land. The response that I sometimes get is, 'Yes, but you are Indian, so how do you know about the tin industry of the past in Cornwall and the communications gateway to the world via cable lines?' I always inform them at this point that I am Indian of origin but not of nationality, and this normally clears the mist of confusion that my colour and appearance cause. It is not racial profiling, in my opinion; it is more to do with having a narrow mind rather than an open one, and that still appears to be the common enemy on both sides of the social domain. I would like to add that I am not stereotyping any particular community, but there is good and bad in everyone. I suppose one can also relate that to social knowledge and education.

One can also criticise the British in India for maintaining linguistic barriers; let's face it, they did not rule the country by speaking Hindi, did they? I do wonder what Enoch would have thought about what I have just written, but I am sure as a colonial he would have put me in my place by letting me know the difference between one who chooses to settle in a land and one who chooses to rule a land. There is a difference and it is a fact that the first thing rulers normally do is implement their language and faith. That is the difference between the British Raj and the Moguls; the British came to rule and not to integrate with society. If they had integrated, then how could they have ruled the place in the manner in which they did? However, there were many British men who did marry Indian women and thus contributed to the society known as Anglo-Indians. At the time it suited British men to have Indian wives and thus forge better relations with the natives in order to pursue the aims of the Raj. There is a myth that in the early days of the British arriving in India they were certain that British women would not have been able to survive pregnancy and the climate out there, so it was more sensible to have Indian wives.

My grandparents came here to integrate, so the onus was on them to learn the linguistic skills and the social interaction skills of the mainstream community of this nation. The British people did not expect us to give up faith or language, but they did have an expectation of etiquette and the usage of language in public.

My maternal grandfather was lucky because he worked in heavy industry in Glasgow and this only contributed towards a very working-class Glaswegian manner of etiquette and language. I always remember him as having an accent that was very strongly Glaswegian and his etiquette was much the same; he would approach a woman by calling her 'hen' or 'doll', and as for men it was either 'big man' or 'wee man'. One can say that it is not standard or appropriate English, but when it came to fitting into local society it was perfect for him and his friends. The language in effect acted as a source of integration; how on earth could he have fed his family if he had not got to grips with the Glaswegian accent and English in general? Because of his slang and funny jokes his personality certainly shone through with the local community. He loved the pub, and I am sure that this was also a major contributing factor to his fitting in so well to the local community. He always said, 'I have a permanent sun tan; that is the only difference between us really, but I am in for a penny and out for a pound, son, just like every working man who needs to get by in any part of the world.'

Enoch himself was not a great integrator with society, and that was not in order to avoid ethnic minority groups. Even at school he was very insular and kept himself to himself in order to achieve and get the best results. How could my grandfather or parents have separated themselves from society when they had to learn about this nation's sights and sounds in a social capacity in order to get by on a daily basis? Their employment prospects and success rates were limited; there was no way my grandfather would have got a job as a bank clerk or government officer, for example, considering he was not brought over to this country for that reason. I am glad that he and the rest did not seclude themselves from society, because it would have filtered down to me and I would not have been able to write this account of how I see Britain today and my place as a British Indian. I do believe that the social education that my parents and grandparents received was of good value because it enabled them to interact with others, and to learn and debate about various issues. I am just glad that I was a participant in those debates that related to the economic and social state of our country during my younger years, and particularly my teenage years.

Enoch's social integration in India was something that only he could have truly commented on because observers always have their own opinion. There is one aspect of his personality that was to be admired, and that was that, despite losing a lot of political allies as a result, he did stand by what he believed in. Believe me, there are some British Asians around this land who have no idea of integration, yet at least Enoch integrated with Indians when he was out in Delhi and other cities during the last stages of the Raj. I have been a victim in social places of gathering where another person of Indian subcontinent origin has seen me and felt as if my presence put his or her social status under threat. Integration can be hindered by the way in which people are taught to integrate. There was an instance in India where an Indian army officer who served for the British was not allowed in an officers' club because of his race. Enoch took great offence at this and decided that it was inappropriate to treat another human like this, so he went off elsewhere with the Indian officer; I am sure that he was the type of man who would have learned something from this officer. We must not forget that this man could speak Urdu to translation level, and one can add Hindi to this because the languages are mutually intelligible.

Enoch Powell was close friends with a Mrs Rose of Pattingham, who was a local Conservative and knew him for over fifty years. She made a comment about her friendship with Enoch and I am sure her account was one of a truthful nature; otherwise she would probably have declined to comment, as most clever politicians do.

Mrs Rose of Pattingham said: '**History has not been kind to Enoch Powell. He was an incredible man and he was not a racist. He gave a speech about the ill treatment of Mau Mau detainees and was a strong Christian.**'

One must ask if his religious conviction had a part to play in his walking out of that officers' club in Pune. I have reason to believe that this was the case because his mother was a strong Christian who taught herself Greek and was close to her faith. From my interaction with people of faith who have studied the Bible I have reached the conclusion that a lot of the impact of what was written in the Bible in Greek was lost through translation. However, Powell was a professor of Greek, so the Greek interpretation of the Bible may have had more impact on him, and this impact could have been reflected in his personality, his attitude to his faith and the practicality of his daily life.

In 1977 Enoch spoke about civil unrest in this nation in an interview, but who he identified as the warring factions was not clear. He did mention the fact that there would be trouble on the streets of Britain because of the immigrant influence. He made it clear that he had changed his mindset with regard to the rate of the increase of immigrants, and that this had dictated his views that had led up to the famous Birmingham speech. He made it equally clear that if the speech had not been made then nothing would have been done to control immigration, and according to him it was something that had to be discussed because it was a huge issue at the time. Enoch did feel that he had underestimated the magnitude of the danger relating to population figures that were estimated to peak by the end of the century. I detected a lot of bitterness towards the Conservative Party in this particular interview; he felt that people were being misled in order to get votes. Nothing new; this was always the plan of any party in government in my own view. Politicians of all parties probably knew that Enoch was right, but there was no way they would have admitted that they agreed with him. Enoch felt as if a civil war was brewing and he had done his job by igniting the spark that led to the funeral pyre of debate being set ablaze. In this interview he made it clear that he would not be blamed for a third of London, Birmingham and Wolverhampton being in a civil war zone because he had done his bit to give the warning.

Many riots have taken place in Britain; one only needs to look at the more recent riots in the summer of 2011 to see how devastating these can be. The riots that happened in Brixton in the early '80s and in Tottenham a few years later could be blamed on race and race relations by some.

One BBC interview will always stay in my memory bank, and that was when the famous writer and broadcaster Darcus Howe was asked questions about the situation in the 2011 London riots. The BBC reporter asked him an inappropriate question: 'You are not a stranger to riots yourself, I understand, are you? You have taken part in them yourself.' This obviously infuriated Howe, and he made it clear that he has never taken part in such activities and demanded that she 'have some respect for an old West Indian Negro'. Although the question was probably innocent and based on a lack of factual knowledge on the reporter's part, it still seemed to imply that generations of black people had always rioted. Surely a person needs to look at the substance of whom they are addressing in a professional capacity. We are all fully aware of the fact that Darcus Howe is very well respected and is a very knowledgeable man, yet on the news report that day the reporter asked the question in a manner that suggested it was just natural for a black man to engage in a riot. During the interview Howe spoke about black and white youths being frustrated with what was happening in the nation, especially with the police stop-and-search checks that black youths had to endure on the streets of London. When he was accused of having taken part in riots in the past it just summed up the nature of the preconceptions the reporter had adopted: preconceptions that the police and other institutions also have when approaching the black community. This was clearly very insulting and I shared the annoyance of Darcus Howe because if I were ever accused of such a thing just because of the fact that I may have been around a riot zone twenty years ago, I too would be very upset. He was quite right in asking for respect due to his ethnicity and race. It was the manner in which the question was asked. If anyone knows who Darcus Howe is, they will have to agree that he did not become successful by rioting. The BBC had to apologise, and rightfully so; it is clearly wrong for anyone to assess someone else based on their age and ethnicity.

I suppose I can look at Diane Abbott with annoyance when she tweeted that 'white people love playing "divide and rule"; we should not play their game'. Surely this also needs to be looked at as a case of applying stereotypes; therefore it is truly evident that it is not just white media and politicians that make verbal errors. Here we have an MP who is well educated and makes similar errors to those who were making statements around Enoch's time in 1968. She also made a statement in 2010 describing David Cameron and Nick Clegg as 'posh white boys from the home counties'. This clearly goes to show that on both sides of the social domain there are serious errors being made in public, in both cases by so-called educated and well-read people. Abbott apologised for her comment relating to the 'divide and rule' issue, which I feel was an inappropriate stereotype of white people. I do wonder what Enoch would have made of her comment. Would he have capitalised on it by blaming it on high levels of immigration, or would he have had a more open mind and tried to investigate where the statement was actually coming from? I believe Enoch would not have made any comment and would have blamed the Conservative Party and the public in an 'I told you so' manner.

Enoch in my view considered the riots of the 1980s to be the outcome of the failure of integration relating to the large numbers of people moving into the country. For the individuals who wanted to blame the Afro-Caribbean community in Brixton for the troubles, Enoch's views were obviously music to their ears. Was Enoch to blame for the riots or were they caused by other aspects of the decade? I believe the riots had more to do with the police relations with the public and the economic situation of the time. What a lot of police officers and racists did not take into account was that the children of the early immigrants had been exposed to a socialisation process that was not about surrendering but about fighting for rights and survival. One only needs to examine how their parents were told at the doorsteps of rented accommodation that no dogs, Irish or blacks were allowed. There was no way that the new generation was going to tolerate this at all.

I believe that these riots happened because times had moved on but not attitudes towards the Afro-Caribbean community, who I believe actually did a lot to revive faith in this nation and bring a new flavour of social rhythm through the introduction of their music and culture into cities like London. Integration was not given a chance to flourish, unlike now when minds have changed on all sides of the social domain.

I do question the equilibrium of social interaction when having to work or socialise with minority groups now carries with it the fear of being branded as a racist; it is now whites who mostly live in fear of being branded as racist, and in many cases it is people of their own ethnicity who measure what is acceptable and what is not. We sadly cannot find a balance between social, humane and political correctness now that we have come so far with establishing good relations in Britain, where institutions like the emergency services and educational establishments have training to deal with cultural and religious sensitivities. We all need to produce equality and diversity plans; even teachers are required to incorporate these issues into their schemes of work. The question that needs to be asked is whether these are becoming solely **tick-box procedures**. If they are, then we are making a mockery of the multicultural Britain that we live in and we are only living in fear of political correctness, leading us to behave like those kids in the video to 'Another Brick in the Wall' by Pink Floyd. They all follow the procedure like robots and are not given any autonomy that releases their true potential and intuition. Different methods of learning through lesson activity are not evident; it is all autocratic, and then at the end the kids riot. I hope we do not head in that direction as a nation, but I do question where we are being led by this system that just cannot find a balance without upsetting the white majority in this country. In my opinion these people are not racist in the majority, but the fear of race is placed in their hearts to keep racial harmony, and in my opinion that is not the way to run a diversely populated nation.

If we look with an open mind at the statement that Enoch made about mass immigration leading to civil war, we can reach the conclusion that the civil war was not just about white people and ethnic minorities. Let's look at the civil unrest in the city of Birmingham that happened in October 2005; there was mass unrest over two nights between British Asians and the predominantly black Afro-Caribbean communities.

Whatever the reason behind these disturbances, one has to ask the question about human behaviour: were Enoch's comments relating to civil unrest just restricted to black and white, or did anyone in his day think of the unrest that could occur between two ethnic communities and that a new type of inter-ethnic disturbance could rock a city such as Birmingham? Surely this was a new challenge for the pro-multiculturalists to deal with. I must add that the press did cover this riot, but if it had been between black and white certain elements of the media would have had a field day. This brings me back to the statement that my grandfather made about certain people profiting from other people's misfortune; there is no doubt that the criminal element from both sides saw an opportunity to prosper from civil unrest. This is something that our nation had to deal with, but if someone were to blame race alone for this issue then I would have to disagree because I blame human behaviour for copycat antics that only escalate such disturbances. It does open questions about the communities that reside in Britain and the challenges that this nation has to deal with. Some may blame immigration; they may return to Enoch's words relating to civil unrest and try to profit in a political sense from his comments that it is the immigrants who appear to cause civil unrest and that they are to blame for all the problems on the streets of inner cities. If someone was born in this nation and that person happens to be participating in a riot and in addition is of ethnic minority origin, it would be wrong to call that person an immigrant. However, those who wish to make it a race issue would call that person an immigrant who is over here rioting and causing trouble.

The famous song 'Ghost Town', released by the well-known band The Specials in the early '80s, reflected the mood amongst the youth. It was evident that the nation was in a mess at the time, with most cities not having much to offer in the way of employment. The music video had both black and white artists in it, and the lyrics of the song expressed the mood at the time; 'people getting angry and no jobs in this country' probably summed up the state of the nation. It is evident that when economic times are good, most are happy and there is no need to point fingers, but in times of economic trouble the blame factor creeps up and finds someone or a group to blame. Again the troublemakers in society would return to Enoch's words, and without actually addressing the issues he spoke about they would capitalise on the infamous words of the Birmingham speech that he made. I am sure Enoch did not want riots in this nation; I believe that his words were aimed more at the government in anger. He was obviously experiencing a deep sense of anxiety and frustration, just like the British black, white and Asian youths that The Specials were referring to in 'Ghost Town'.

The programmes on television at the time also depicted the feelings of British Asians towards white British people. The series *It Ain't Half Hot Mum* acted as a reminder to Asians of who was in charge of them during the Empire. It only brought back bad memories for those who lived under the British Raj in India, but those less open-minded white people probably took from it a sense of authority over the immigrants working in the Wolverhampton factories. It is obvious that Britain had left terrible poverty in India when it had departed, but then again after the war with Germany Britain did not have much left in the bank account to be proud of. It was this dire poverty that probably made people come from India to Britain; then again, Britain also needed to get back on its feet in the post-war years, and what better way to do it than by attracting cheap labour?

Mind Your Language was another series that brought a lot of laughter to all communities in Britain, and that included the Asians because at the time they were happy to see Asians on television. Stereotypes do make people laugh, but they also have the opposite effect by creating a long-term perception of a race that can be passed from one generation to the next; that is the danger. *Mind Your Language* was intended to make people laugh, but it did show Asians and other foreign people as objects of laughter. At the time Asians in Britain were facing some very serious problems in the form of racism in the workplace and in public, so in all honesty the media portrayal was questionable. As someone who is from Scotland I must say the makers of the series were fair in their method of highlighting the issues surrounding accents; there was an episode where they brought in a Scot who just could not be understood and he had to sit in a class with foreigners to learn English. It goes to show that stereotypes can spare no one when they are in full swing.

I do believe that the producers of these shows were actually trying to educate people in a way, using stereotypes to highlight the wrong way of dealing with people. *Till Death Us Do Part*, starring the one and only Warren Mitchell, was a classic example of portraying stereotypes. Mitchell's character did not like anyone, and he was the type of man that one would want to avoid because it would just be too hard to get anything through the wall of ignorance. I still watch the shows of the '70s and '80s and I feel as if I am laughing at the lack of social awareness and the closed-mindedness of these characters who view the world in terms of stereotypes.

If the producers intended to highlight the social ignorance of people like Alf Garnett then they succeeded, because I find the acting to be good and the character's portrayal certainly exposes the behaviour of certain people in society who hinder social integration and harmony. I will never forget the episode of *Till Death Us Do Part* where Alf Garnett tried to convince his daughter that there were no black people in the Bible and that therefore blacks were inferior to whites. This clearly shows the ignorance of the character, but even this scene needs to be looked at in a serious light because, behind the laughter at his ignorance, one can see that scenes like this can create a hindrance to real-life social integration. How would a black person feel if the next day, in the playground or workplace, they were told that they were no Christian because Alf Garnett made it clear that there are no blacks in the Bible?

In the same series Alf had a 'right old go' at the miners as well as black people, so really it was a social education to watch *Till Death Us Do Part*. There is no way that it would be shown today, but I believe that this series did a lot to open minds and make people aware of how wrong it is to have an attitude that destroys the potential for social progress and harmony. Both elements of society, open- and closed-minded, can make something out of this statement. Sadly, when one is made to feel inferior, social integration does face hindrances.

I do believe that accents that had a tone of the Indian sub-continent to them were instrumental to the success of certain shows in past decades, but nowadays there is no way British Asians like me could even speak like the first immigrants because we have British accents and we just do not fit into the mould of the Asian characters portrayed by these shows. **Who would we be making a mockery out of, if we attempted to play one of these characters? Ourselves, seeing that we are British and would be pretending to be someone we are not.**

If one were to state that these shows were a hindrance to social interaction for minorities they could possibly be right to an extent. However, I felt as if the shows were highlighting bigoted characters that quite clearly were visible in society and it was they who were mainly being laughed at for their social inadequacies and ignorance, rather than the people against whom they were prejudiced.

A major hindrance to social interaction is always the ignorance of people, and this is evident in many walks of life. I would like to ask the question of whether people were ignorant of Enoch's views. It is obvious that the character of Alf Garnett was very ignorant about the views of others in society, and this ignorance was also evident in real life from a political and social perspective.

MK Gandhi once said, '**Many people, especially ignorant people, want to punish you for speaking the truth, for being correct, for being you. Never apologise for being correct, or for being years ahead of your time. If you're right and you** know it, speak your mind. Even if you are a minority of one, the truth is still the truth.'

There is no doubt that Enoch spoke his mind very well indeed. The statement that Gandhi made was an expression of democracy and freedom; Enoch, in all his public debates and discussions, was only implementing his freedom of speech. If we are now to ridicule him, many years later, then are we to be found guilty of being ignorant of the need for democracy and freedom of speech? It is true that there are many hindrances towards social interaction and integration, and it is now clear that democracy itself can play a role in the birth of ignorance towards different people, but anger only breeds anger and that can be managed by society and governments if the power of speech cannot.

I do believe Enoch was ahead of his time and I also believe very strongly that he was someone who placed his nationality and English nature at the centre of his views. Sometimes in life one has to learn to give as well as take. His very own education was dictated by foreign cultures like the Romans and the Greeks, so one would have reached the conclusion that he was accepting of different cultures. However, the question for debate is this: what particular cultures and races of people was he really in awe of? The cultures that he saw as being superior to his very own Britain, and the ones that in his view contributed towards the development of the world? He certainly did seem to perceive a hierarchy of cultures and certain races based on their historical achievements on an international colonial scale; there is a connection here with his desire to become the Viceroy of India, a role in which his colonial views would have been very applicable. It is rumoured that when Britain lost India in 1947 Enoch walked around the streets in a state of sorrow. I believe that this loss was a great sadness to him, but was this a love affair of one-way dominance rather than a mutual attraction? I believe it is fair to say that Enoch saw British rule as the best way that a nation like India could be governed, and therefore saw India's desire for independence as a mass show of disrespect to the British state and its rule in India. Enoch himself did like the nation and wanted to play a significant role in British India; he truly did see that land as one that would have placed him in history as a man of greatness. His love for history was such that I believe he really wanted to make his mark in history, so that the name Powell could be associated with greatness and power.

CHAPTER FIVE

Multiculturalism, Identity, Immigration and the EU

My vision for Britain is for all the peoples of our nation to be united in a sense of patriotic pride. This was the intention of my grandparents who came to this land in the 1940s to contribute towards the reconstruction of Britain after the war.

It is with regret that I get called Indian even though my nationality is British; I am not ashamed of my Indian ethnicity, but there is a distinct difference between my nationality and ethnicity. I prefer to be known as British, or if someone wants to put a fine point on the issue they can call me British of Indian origin. I feel that my ethnicity and nationality are two very different issues that have sadly over the years been blended into confusion by those who pursue the multicultural agenda and political correctness scaremongering. I, like others in our nation, am very disappointed in the vision that Conservative and Labour governments have had for diversity and cultural awareness.

As someone who has been teaching in further education for years, it has become very apparent to me that there is an issue with the understanding of the multicultural ethos. If there is one person in the class who happens to be different then there is a requirement to change one's teaching strategies and ensure that one is not being **Britcentric** in one's teaching. I am all for treating people equally; I have nothing against equality and treating people in a fair and democratic manner. However, there is a problem and it is becoming a hindrance to our integration in this nation. I was once asked to teach a class of legal secretarial students and I really felt that there was a massive problem with the recruitment of these young women. They were mainly from Eastern Europe and their English was exceptionally weak, yet they were placed onto this course to ensure that there was multicultural representation visible in the class. Those young women really struggled to learn because they did not have a basic grasp of our language, yet each time I complained about this I was told that I did not have cultural awareness! The rules of the multiculturalists actually made these students suffer more than they would have otherwise because they were not ready for such a linguistic challenge.

We have become so scared of offending people that we have allowed uncertainty to develop; teachers and others in public service are not really clear about the multicultural agenda. Some maths teachers have really struggled to understand how to involve cultural awareness when teaching students how to do fractions. This has caused so much panic that it has resulted in certain teachers being afraid of doing their job in case they are accused of not being multicultural enough in the classroom. On the other side of the equation there is very little emphasis on teaching people of different ethnic groups about the 'majority cultures' of the United Kingdom; I am referring to Scotland, England, Northern Ireland and Wales. When I was at school I learned a lot about the Scottish Islands and the history of Britain; we learned about the Victorians and we were shown educational documentaries at a young age about how the Victorians lived and what they did for us. If this were promoted today it would be looked upon as too Britcentric, and if a lecturer were enthusiastic about the British countryside and used that enthusiasm to drive the teaching process then he or she would be looked upon as a failure when being evaluated against the equality and diversity criteria.

Multiculturalism in my opinion has failed this society. It let itself get hijacked by political correctness and by the people who wanted to pursue political correctness and use it as a resource of fear to place in the hearts and minds of the Great British people. If anything it has only gagged democracy and free speech in this nation, and I believe that I am a victim of it.

I remember my city being given the status of European City of Culture when I was younger. Even as a teenager I was critical of this status, because we still had so much work to do to clean up the sectarian issue that was causing so much grief amongst the Rangers and Celtic faithful of Glasgow, but we were still jumping for joy at being granted the status of European City of Culture. When one looks at the state of Britain today, one can see that multiculturalism has still not achieved much at all to be proud of. If we look at Kent we can see there is a huge division between areas like Gravesend and Sevenoaks; the economic and social divide is truly immense. The majority of people who live in Sevenoaks have had no experience of any real integration with people of minority ethnic origin and, to be frank about this, they have had little exposure to different ethnic groups. If one asks the ethnic minorities of Gravesend if they have ever visited Sevenoaks, the answer normally is, 'What for? My community is here, and so are my work and family.' Surely one has to ask oneself the question of whether multiculturalism has failed this society if two societies that live less than forty minutes' drive apart know very little about each other. If the multiculturalists call this a success one only needs to ask what a failure looks like.

Self-imposed segregation still happens where people buy homes to be close to their 'own kind', in the sense of ethnicity rather than nationality. As a society we are still engaged in a form of segregation that is not apartheid in the generally accepted sense but certainly is divisional in a social sense. Political correctness and the categorisations of ethnic status created by the multiculturalists have only contributed towards this way of living.

The other issue of concern for me is that there is another wave of immigrants coming into our nation who have had little exposure to our history and have little knowledge about our way of life. It is easy to learn about these areas in such a modern age of technology; however, due to our exceptional tolerance in this nation there is no real requirement for anyone who comes from a European land to learn about us.

European Union immigration has also caused a new wave of integration problems. A lot of minority groups feel that they have been the victims of more racial abuse from immigrants from Eastern Europe than from their own fellow British citizens. The European Union was so busy in trying to integrate all of us that it completely forgot about the status of Britain's history with its Commonwealth and people. This is the aspect of cultural integration that hurts me the most: the issue surrounding Britain and its Commonwealth. The citizens of the Commonwealth fought so hard for the freedom of Europe, but it was not Britain that let them down in the end; it was the European Union. As a union of nations it completely ignored Britain's status as the Head of the Commonwealth, and the people of ethnic minority origin whose families came from lands such as the Indian subcontinent and the West Indies got completely ignored along with the white British citizens. Our traditions, values and heritage were ignored in favour of the determination of the pro-Europeans to mould this island into a wider United States of Europe. Our Commonwealth was looked upon as second-class by the European Union, and the people who came from Commonwealth lands and contributed towards the freedom of Europe were totally ignored by this union.

Multiculturalism should have been left to individual communities to promote. If someone has the desire to learn about someone else's culture, it should be purely down to them as an individual to learn about it. At present the nation does not really allow people to opt out of learning about other cultures and in my view this is very unfair. If we feel that we are learning about a culture that is not conducive to our way of life or has anti-democratic values, we are still expected to have the teaching of these cultures imposed upon us. If we as people choose not to learn about certain cultures then we get accused of being racist, and this in my view is the autocratic arm of those in the political correctness hierarchy being exercised. If multiculturalism had been left to schools and universities to integrate into their own learning without government interference, it may have been a good addendum to the learning objectives. However, it was **hijacked** and **imposed** upon the people of this land.

Sadly too many people have become afraid to speak about the issues that affect our society because they do not know what social, political or legal rule they may be breaking, and this is not good for the future of local or national democracy in this nation. Another issue that causes me concern is the way names get changed in this country to suit the agenda of the political correctness brigade; a fine example is the change of name from the Royal Ulster Constabulary to the Police Service of Northern Ireland. Surely we cannot go around allowing these sorts of changes to take place when they do not deal with or tackle any of the real problems that people face in society. My grandparents came to the United Kingdom of Great Britain and Northern Ireland, and if this name is too imposing for people then they surely must consider whether this is truly the nation for them. My family have never had an issue with the Union Jack or its place in our society. If I were abroad and I had lost my passport and wallet, I would be more than happy to see the British embassy with a Union Jack flying from its rooftop. If someone is insulted by this then one has to examine where this response is coming from and the problems that this school of thought brings to integration and having a sense of national pride and belonging.

I recently went back to my old school in Glasgow and I called the school afterwards to thank them for the visit; they just wanted to make me aware of how proud they were of the forty different languages that were being spoken in the school and the exceptionally multicultural nature of the school.

Nobody seemed to want to discuss the real issues facing students and the cost of further education, or the stress and strain put onto teachers who have to deal with classes where many languages are being spoken. It is sad that the face of multiculturalism is smiling at us in mockery because we are all confused about what it is trying to achieve for us. I went to school and I did religious education; I had normal classes with my classmates and I faced no malicious racism at my secondary school. I have excellent memories of my school and the teachers; we all learned about Scottish culture and British culture without anyone displaying an imposing nature and we all got on very well indeed. We were proud of our city, our school and our nation. Sadly now there is a lot of emphasis on the misconception of what culture actually stands for in Britain. I love places like Cornwall, but sadly very little knowledge about this place is shared in our schools. Yet it is Cornwall from where the first telecommunications were sent out by cable to the whole world. What is wrong in teaching and learning about this famous British place and the contribution it made to the world? Surely it is knowledge that we should be proud of regardless of ethnicity or labels that have been imposed upon us.

This is the most frustrating part of the confusion that surrounds multiculturalism; it does not allow autonomy, and it is implemented in such a way that we are not allowed to be democratic when dealing with the multiculturalists' requirements. We must not speak about uniculturalism, as it is seen as imposing. How charming this appears to be, considering this is all coming from those who support multiculturalism. If one is a uniculturalist, one sees equality in national identity and promotes values that are in accordance with the place where we live. Someone like me who is of British nationality and of ethnic minority origin would support the values of uniculturalism, an approach that, as I see it, has more **equality** and **democracy** attached to it.

Multiculturalism can sometimes turn on people who want

to change their faith and culture. I know many people who are of Indian origin and have changed their faith from Sikhism and Hinduism to Christianity. Those people are not generally welcomed into the multicultural domain; they become outcasts and have little involvement in the affairs of the community. I ask myself what multiculturalism does to protect those people who wish to exercise the values of British democracy. There is far too much confusion between culture and religion; for example the perception is that if your family is from the Punjab in India then you must be Sikh or Hindu. Multiculturalists focus on the majority faiths of these lands and engage with them to add value to the multicultural local agenda that is always pursued by the local authority. If, however, one is a Christian Roman Catholic and one's family originally came from the Punjab over fifty years ago, then the mainstream ethnic **'majority'** take first place in social integration conducted by the multiculturalists. Is this fair to the one who shares the same colour and cultural values but is left behind based on faith because he or she is seen as different by others who share the same ethnic origin? **The majority of local authorities themselves are engaging in discrimination against the minorities within a minority group, and this is all being conducted under the guise of multiculturalism.**

One also needs to look at the disastrous importation of the caste system into this country from the Indian subcontinent. This is a brutal form of social apartheid where one is classified by one's family's social class based on employment and education; it is open to some of the most horrendous violations of human rights. It was imported into the United Kingdom and multiculturalists did nothing to stop this form of social apartheid entering our nation; in fact, it somehow managed to blend into their very own multicultural activities.

The 'equality and diversity' agenda imposes inequality by imposing different rules for different people, as well as discriminating against the smallest minority, which can be one individual in any institution. Diversity itself can be distorted by creating set client groups and removing the liberties that make us diverse, which is a very British thing. If one looks at town twinning and examines the justification for it, there is evidence that client groups must be catered for. In the city of Glasgow there is a large population of people of Pakistani origin; the city council twinned Glasgow with Lahore in Pakistan simply because of this large population. The council states that it treats all community groups equally; however this is not equality in my view and the view of many others, because there is a huge gulf of a difference socially and economically between the two cities. The people of Glasgow gain no benefit from this partnership; if one were to approach those of Indian or Jewish origin who settled in the city in the early part of the last century, they clearly would have no links with the city of Lahore. **If someone from Glasgow is a Christian of Pakistani origin, how would he or she feel about a twinning partnership that is not justified in their view due to the fact that many Christians of Pakistani origin are trying to flee Pakistan due to persecution? Does this type of equality and diversity that has been reflected through town twinning partnership suit them?**

The same happened in Gravesend, Kent, where the city of Jalandhar in Punjab, India, was twinned up with Gravesend based on the fact that many Gravesend residents are from the Sikh faith and originally come from this city in Punjab. What **quantitative** and **qualitative** measures were taken to establish which economically deprived communities would benefit from this partnership? In all truthfulness these twinnings are just to appease the multicultural and diversity ethos focusing on the '**majority**' minority groups in both places, Glasgow and Gravesend. It is truly just appeasement and a publicity campaign that shows that the government's equality and diversity aims are being met through a so-called multicul-tural partnership. If one were to look at Gravesend and Jalandhar in more depth, one would clearly see that Jalandhar has a huge **child labour** problem. This means, for me and other British citizens of this town, that our Great British nationalities have been associated with **child labour** through forced appeasement of the multicultural, equality and diversity tick-boxes that local authorities wish to subscribe to and promote.

What I have found to be very embarrassing is the way in which it is considered non-acceptable to have a discussion. I speak about controlling immigration and the preservation of Britain and its Commonwealth, I ask my white friends to engage and they say they could lose their jobs if they as much as comment. This is what has happened to us; multicultural-ism has made people feel so guilty that their democratic right to speak about the nation and its future has been silenced. Surely this is a disaster for race relations and integration. Multiculturalists and political correctness have allowed people not to engage and promote their skills in the usage of the English language. So many people complain that in most British towns and cities they hear Eastern European languages being spoken and fear for the future of the British language known as English. If we want people to truly integrate and have a sense of belonging, we need to push our language to the centre of the social domain and allow that to be the language of all official forms and appointments that are made. Immi-grants and others will not see the need to integrate if there is no requirement to do so. My parents speak English and they also speak their ethnic mother tongue language, as do I; however, I do not expect the people of this land to change their practices of engagement to suit the whole world, because we too are part of this world and need to be recognised as such.

Britain needs to change and so does the tolerance of its people; all of its great people must come together and demand that the method by which multiculturalism is imposed upon us by local councils, education authorities and politicians must change for the values of this nation to be shared and celebrated. Nobody would be happier than my family and I if we were brought back into British society in a

unicultural manner that can see our Britishness and not our imposed identities.

During the 1960s it is evident that Irish, black and Asian communities faced a lot of racism; there were also many cases of humanity displayed by the mainstream British public towards these minority groups. It is very sad that there was very little gratitude for and recognition of the effort that was made during both wars by ethnic minorities, and although there is no doubt that now there is recognition, it took a long time for this recognition to be achieved. Too much emphasis was placed on segregation rather than integration, and I believe that it must have been very hard indeed for those early settlers from Ireland, the Indian subcontinent and the West Indies to become part of this land because of the bigoted racists who made their lives extremely difficult. There is no doubt that many people from white and ethnic minority backgrounds did a lot to tackle the issue of racism in society during the '50s and '60s. I ask where the recognition of those efforts is now. Political correctness has made it very difficult for the people of this country to regain that cohesion and work towards unity of nationality. This is what we as a nation really need to achieve. The essential mechanism of our nationality needs to work with the components of our society in order to celebrate a sense of Britishness that makes us all feel very proud of our achievements over the years.

In the 2001 census, 71% of people within the United Kingdom stated that they are Christian, and faith schools do make up a large part of our education. I do not want to see the elimination of any faith school or radically change the appearance of people who wish to wear the crucifix or a turban. We must maintain freedom of speech, and the freedom to perform religious activities must be allowed to continue as long as those activities are not hindering the morals and principles of the mainstream culture of this land. It is the management of multiculturalism that has been distorted over the years; I have met many people who feel that they must hide their faith because it is looked upon as imposing or in some cases offensive. As a British citizen of ethnic minority origin I do not believe that my culture must take priority over anybody else's culture; however, I would like to have the freedom to manage how I conduct my culture. I do not need a local authority or education authority to take control of any community's culture. The job of the authorities is to provide local services for all communities, not to change their delivery plan to keep a certain community happy; that does not reflect equality. If a community wishes to promote its culture to other people in society, I believe that it can at its own expense and under its own management. This allows democracy and ownership to take place without any interference from local authorities who pick and choose what cultures to promote and then believe they can impose the ethos of political correctness upon us.

Enoch Powell made the statement, '**Let it go on until the civil war comes.**' These are very serious words and can place a lot of fear in the hearts and minds of people who live in Great Britain. However, the nation does seem to be at '**social war**' with the concept of political correctness and multiculturalism. There is no doubt that something has gone wrong with the way the academics in our society have implemented a social structure and doctrine that have become a hindrance to our daily lives and integration.

In 1976 Enoch Powell made a speech about the loss of national status for the British nation as a direct result of Britain being part of the EEC. The central and political issue surrounding identity obviously caused him great concern because identity is very important to every nation. National identity is far more important than cultural identity; however, our institutions did not focus on national identity, and sadly the focus was instead on identity based on culture. It made us all feel that being patriotic was something that was looked upon as very radical and extreme. Now we have discovered that when we want to be known as British, it is a hindrance because we have to declare ourselves as being non-racist and then British in order to qualify as being a Great British national. We have become a community of communities; is this how we want to be classified or known? What is wrong with being known as British regardless of ethnicity?

In the '80s and '90s I came across so many people who felt as if they were European and not British. I have never met anyone in Asia who calls him or herself an Asian; they regard their nationality as being their identity. Multiculturalism has allowed us to walk into the path of segregation and has separated us from the colour of our passport. We focus more on the colour of skin and ethnic backgrounds before we assess national status as being British.

Enoch was concerned about immigration figures of **50,000** per annum and now we have an even greater number, which according to Migration Watch UK is a major concern. In 1997 the incoming figure was **50,000**; this figure increased to **250,000** by 2010. Nearly **four million imigrants** have entered the UK since 1997. It clearly shows that we cannot continue with the principles of multiculturalism because it cannot be managed. The EU itself has given no regard to Britain and has allowed freedom of movement to hinder our social, economic and political progress. We are not a free people; we are tied to an institution that clearly does not understand Britain or its Commonwealth. We are losing our national identity due to the EU being a hindrance to our affairs and meddling in our internal politics. There is a war of words going on and this will result in something having to surrender; either we divorce ourselves from this relationship or we lose all that we have in relation to our identity and national status.

The British people have been tricked and cheated out of their inheritance of self-government. Even well-established ethnic minorities feel that immigration from Eastern Europe is far too great for this nation to control and it is now causing a stereotypical statement that we hear every day: '**Too many foreigners in this town!**' A lot of ethnic minorities now feel that multiculturalism has done nothing to stop them from being called 'foreigners'. I know so many ethnic minorities who oppose this European immigration open-door policy due to concern about employment and social issues. During Enoch's time it was the white British people who felt as if this applied to them, and now all British nationals regardless of colour are complaining and showing concern over mass immigration from Europe. Sadly, because multiculturalism did not promote national identity, we are not united in the opposition to the shackles that have been placed on us. Now we want to be united and there is a problem. I have been told that I am a foreigner who should not be concerned about EU immigration because we are now a multicultural society and under this system we are not allowed to complain; I had to explain that as a British national I am very concerned about this and I will not surrender to any smokescreen. It is exactly this smokescreen that has caused all the confusion about 'legal immigration' into Britain. We are not allowed to question anything because it seems that we are all meant to be a happy nation under the banner of multiculturalism and if we complain we are being prejudiced and going against the grain; **this has completely obscured our national identity and vision for the future.**

Enoch Powell made a speech relating to the EEC in 1976 and referred to those who were weak-willed; he said, '**We ought always to be on our guard against those who … whisper in our ear, "It's done now and cannot be undone." For these are commonly the voices of cowardice.'**

Democracy allows change, and I believe that all British nationals regardless of cultural or ethnic identities must unite and become British in order to work for the better future of this nation. If we continue to allow ourselves to be divided by multiculturalism and political correctness, we will soon lose our national unity and we will all sit back and think about the colonial 'divide and rule' ethos that has now been imposed upon all British people. No nation can be held against its will in relation to self-governance and independence; we allowed ourselves to become mad in confusion and national identity and lost our title deeds to national independence. Britain was hijacked by the European Communities Act in 1972 by deception and its Commonwealth was severed from an economic perspective. Sadly we could not unite because of social division and segregation, and now that we have third-generation British nationals who feel more multicultural than British we are being held as a hostage by the EU. Surely one would have to ask what takes more priority in the defence of democratic values: culture or nationality. I would rather defend this land with my national identity than with my culture, because within my culture I am insular, but within my national identity I am united in cohesion with my fellow citizens without any regulations or barriers imposed upon me.

I truly agree with Enoch Powell's views regarding political integration with Europe. There is no doubt that his speech made us realise that there is scope for debate and immigration is something that needs to be discussed amongst our communities. However, now we are facing a new wave of immigration and the challenges that it imposes upon us. Many people of ethnic origin are now sharing the views of Enoch Powell and feel that their identity is also being put into question over this new wave of legal immigration. So many people feel that this is an issue, and sadly the Birmingham speech that Enoch Powell made only silenced the debate relating to immigration for well over forty years!

I do agree that the selection of words that he used was inappropriate and caused a lot of problems for innocent Asians and West Indians who really just wanted to settle here and contribute towards Britain. It hurts me a lot to listen to the words of the speech that he made because a man of his linguistic calibre could easily have used straight-to-the-point statements without being offensive. I can see why at the time he used the words that he did; during the '60s there were many people who felt that British supremacy and world domination was alive and well, and this obviously was reflected through the language of domination. On the other hand, I do not have a problem with the way he addressed the European issue and the words that he used when he made speeches about Europe and its political domination over my Great Britain.

Enoch Powell has left me with a double perception of his charisma and way of thinking; I cannot hide the fact that I love the English language and his usage of English truly was of a charismatic nature. However, my grandfather, who came here in the '40s and wanted to be an integral part of this nation, found himself on the receiving end of the interpretation of the words that Enoch Powell used in his speech. Surely it was unfair on Enoch's part to speak in a manner that could have resulted in mass violence breaking out; he could have used words that were more in line with the objective of dealing with immigration and the problems that can arise from not controlling it. He did speak about ethnic minorities in a very stereotypical way; however, I do agree that he was right to raise the issue and discuss immigration in full. The manner of the speech was very questionable indeed with respect to his use of language; I am sure with his personal lexicon he could have raised his points in a more appropriate manner and not left a legacy that only focuses on the Birmingham speech. Sadly people only refer to that speech when his name is mentioned; he failed to create a suitable equilibrium to his legacy in his many speeches, which in my view were excellent in terms of the English that was used and the way in which he made his point. I have been told by people in Wolverhampton who remember him that he was a truly fantastic MP and was very efficient indeed; one can only respect that side of the man.

Immigration at the time of the Birmingham speech was in the face of the British people and it was visible in towns and cities; this allowed his speech to be persuasive amongst white working communities like the dockers in London who walked out of work in support of Enoch Powell. Had EU immigration and regulations been in full flight like they are today, I am sure that Enoch Powell would still have had a strong impact on

British nationalism. He would have been welcomed by many British citizens today if he had made a speech about the EU and the hindrances that it has caused Britain socially, politically and financially. I am sure that many ethnic minorities would have supported him in the quest to free Britain from the EU. The question is how would he have looked upon Eastern European immigrants? Many still believe that white immigration does not get noticed as much as Asian or black immigration; I am sure that this is the case because if someone looks different they obviously get noticed more, thus drawing more attention to figures.

I honestly believe that in the present day Enoch Powell would have made a similar speech without the controversy and he would have managed to take the lead in dealing with the European issue and the financial implications that it has brought to Britain. His form of British nationalism would have fitted in very well indeed today amongst British citizens regardless of ethnic origin.

If we are to be integrated as a society we firstly need to be in touch with our nation; if we are not in touch with our nation we cannot design or build a vision. Enoch Powell was working in accordance with the interests of this nation with his disapproval of European membership. His vision of Europe has certainly developed into realistic fruition with many of our people who now look back and state that he was right about many issues that we face today. Most who agree with him also state that they do not agree with his usage of words but they do with the ethos of his intentions for Britain. He certainly gave inevitabilities a good shake in his day, but I would have liked to see him in action today in Brussels, fighting for the interests of Britain by using words that are not derogatory or directed towards one particular race. I would have been the first to have joined him in the quest to fight for Britain's freedom from political union with Europe! I certainly would not have been standing next to him when he made the Birmingham speech because I do not use the colour of skin to achieve a political point by appealing to the lowest common denominator. I do believe that he had every right to make his speech under the rules of freedom of speech; however, as someone who held his position in society, he did have a responsibility to keep the peace whilst raising his point of view. Sadly that peace was not maintained, resulting in more divisions being created, and for me Britain is about being unified, not divided.

Some in Britain today would say that history is repeating itself, specifically the immigration of the '50s and '60s. One needs to examine the political and economic differences of the decades; in the '50s and '60s Britain was not paying billions into the EEC and did not face immigration that was in the hundreds of thousands per annum. History is not repeating itself because the climate is political, economic and social. It is a totally different type of resentment that exists against high levels of immigration today. In Enoch's day it was probably more of a racial issue and fear of job loss; today it is more a case of not being in control of our nation's decision-making and parliamentary ownership than a matter of race. We have moved on from race and now are focusing upon the interests of the nation and its economic position. We are more pragmatic about the situation and do not rely on the propaganda of scaremongering; we have obviously moved on from the '50s and '60s.

I do agree that we are being put under a lot of pressure today because of mass immigration and an open-door policy dictated by the EU. This is not fair on all British nationals because we can only manage so much. We cannot have uncontrolled immigration; we need an element of control that we are in charge of, and the present state of affairs does not allow us to be in control of our nation. If I were to be accused of sounding like Enoch Powell or having the views of some of the white population of Enoch's day, I would have to emphatically disagree. My views as an ethnic minority individual are purely for the interests of Britain; this is my country and I am proud of it, therefore surely I should have an equal say in the policies relating to our self-control, economic status and immigration numbers.

It is evident that there are many people from Eastern Europe who have been caught by **'social surprise'** by the ethnic makeup of our nation. I myself have been asked many times by people from Eastern Europe why I see myself as a British citizen. This has obviously caused some distress because I see myself as being a citizen of this nation and here I am being questioned by someone who is not a citizen of this land. This mode of thinking cannot qualify as being racist, but it is a point of reality that we must counter-attack because we have a duty to defend the Commonwealth history that we have and the people with Commonwealth ancestry who live here because of that heritage.

There is obviously anxiety for the future in my mind because it has taken us years to get to this stage of acceptance relating to nationality and ethnicity through sound integration. Here we are now, not only having to explain ourselves but having to start all over again to accommodate those who come from nations that belong to the EU, which never showed any regard towards our Commonwealth and the social fabric of Great Britain.

Yes, it is fair to say that we are rebelling as a nation against this imposed policy of open-door immigration and it is also fair to say that we are showing a lot of apathy towards our government. The difference between today and Enoch's day is one of unity from a social perspective; anti-European thoughts are being expressed by British nationals from all backgrounds. Our new issue of immigration is not restricted just to white people showing anger or disappointment; it is now affecting society on a broader spectrum. Young people in particular are now looking towards a solution to the mass unemployment that has been imposed upon them by rules and regulations; these regulations were first imposed upon their grandparents, but the descendants are now paying the price for them by having to surrender to cheap labour from Eastern Europe. This affects all British nationals now, whereas back in Enoch's time it was more an issue of only white people looking to defend their society and employment.

Enoch defined two categories of immigrant when speaking about how he wanted to manage immigration. The first category related to those who wanted to come here and work or train, and the other category related to those who came here to settle in high numbers and cause a problem to the state. The manner in which Enoch Powell was looking at this situation clearly demonstrated that he had no problem with people coming here if they had something to offer this nation by working in the fields of medicine and nursing.

We are making the same point today with Eastern European immigration. We are now finding ourselves stating that we want controlled immigration and we want fewer people to come and settle here because immigration is far too much of a strain on the nation's health, housing and education services. We are returning to the points that Enoch was making; the only differences are that we have become more tolerant and we have not been able to do much because of our association with the European Union. Frustration has been building up amongst the British people and now we are at the point where we want to do something about immigration, but we feel that we cannot in case we offend or get on the wrong side of political correctness; **this in my opinion has allowed the problem to escalate.**

Enoch Powell clearly had an issue with Commonwealth immigration, and I believe that because it was Commonwealth immigration the race debate was at the centre of the discussions at the time. In today's Britain it is not so much race as it is space that is causing the problem in society; the big issue that we are facing with immigration is that we are not in control of the numbers that are coming from the EU. I do agree with Enoch Powell's statement that the numbers have to be practical. If the numbers are practical we can have an element of control, and we can use this to ensure that we create a social equilibrium that is fair to the existing population of this land and fair to the numbers of immigrants coming into this country. We are presently engaged in allowing unlimited numbers to come in; do we have the jobs to offer these people? We have to be fair to people coming to Britain; if we have far too many people in a land with nothing to offer to them, **how can we be called sensible by other nations?** We are creating a problem for the existing British nationals and the people whom we have allowed to come in to the country. We are grinding the gears of the engine, not allowing the engine to drive towards social and economic sensibility.

Enoch Powell spoke about social unrest; our behaviour at present relating to immigration is creating unrest in an economic and equality sense. We as a nation pride ourselves upon equality in so many aspects of our functionality, but in the case of immigration we are presenting and delivering so much inequality because we have no mandate to act in the interest of our nation, instead serving the imposed immigration mandate of the EU upon our people and nation.

The ethos of integration has only caused greater segregation in the fields of employment and social interaction. We are clearly seeing Britain as a place that has no independence, and without this key element of democracy we are finding ourselves disillusioned with politics; apathy amongst the public towards politics and politicians has increased. The people of this nation are now being separated from the public debate relating to the EU because of years of tolerance towards the EU. It is very strange that the people of this nation did not question the financial losses that we made as a result of being in the EU, but when the immigration increased all of a sudden the people of this nation looked towards the politicians to stem the tide of people coming into Britain. It is apparent that when change happens that affects the pound in the pocket, employment, prices on the high street and visible immigration in British towns and cities, it becomes an issue that needs to be dealt with fast.

Enoch spoke about the implications of our being in the EEC and the common agricultural policy being a massive issue for Britain; he made a speech relating to the EEC and he said, '**The common agricultural policy does not suit our requirements.**' How can we measure the length of our requirements when our independence as a nation has been taken away from us? Enoch also said, 'The very principle of a common agricultural policy, which is the foundation ... and the one functioning reality of the EEC today, is ... a regime totally incompatible with the requirements of a densely populated, highly industrialised island nation. It is something that the EEC cannot change and will not change, which is why I must part company with the Prime Minister.'

Enoch said that when a nation is not in control of its borders or fisheries, which, may I add, form a very crucial part of an island nation's economy, then it clearly is being suffocated of its very own autonomy; **I can only agree with him on this issue of self-control.**

The common man or woman clearly is not benefiting from this union that is now causing an impediment to the national existence and independence of Britain itself. We have become a nation that is a province of Europe, and the British electorate in small things and great things alike is being led towards an ethos of unity with a European Union that clearly has separated us from the rest of the world and greater commercial opportunities. The struggle over Britain's political independence will be a struggle that we will not win unless we unite to become a nation that is self-sufficient in decision-making, that deals with its own regulations and that has self-control at every stage of its status as a nation, both internal and external. If one is a patriot one needs to be associated with a nation; our former leaders and present leaders are not patriotic because they are dismantling the sovereignty of this nation by allowing a uniform EU that does not allow us to be proud of who and what we are.

Let's look at self-control from a social perspective. If we

allow high numbers of people to enter this nation and have no control over the qualifications and skills that would enhance our labour market, then what favours are we doing for our economy? There is no way the EU would allow us to impose regulations upon someone coming from Western, Central or Eastern Europe; we would not be allowed to do such a thing to enhance the quality of the people that we attract into this nation. If we are not even allowed to have this type of control, then what is the point of having a puppet government that surrenders the '**common sense**' policies that the British people really want?

Back in Enoch's time in Wolverhampton, one would have raised the question of translators and other associated costs with immigration. We have a much greater problem today where in London and other British cities the English language is not at the centre of daily discourse at home or in society. People who come from certain nations in Europe have no requirement to learn the language before they come here; however, an Indian author who writes clearly in perfect English needs to prove that he or she is fluent in the language. Is this fair to the people of the Commonwealth? Yes, I agree people should be able to speak the language, but should we have one rule for one and another rule for an EU national who does not need to speak a word of English but can come and settle here? **This clearly goes to show that we as a nation are being made to look like we are being discriminatory when we quite frankly do not intend to be.** Because we are being controlled by an EU that places its interests before Britain's interests, we are perceived to be in the wrong by non-EU nations. When our government wants to convince us it is doing something about immigration, it imposes rules upon *non*-EU nationals. The problem is immigration from the EU, but the government always distracts our attention from the EU and returns our focus upon Commonwealth immigration to give us the feeling that something constructive is happening.

CHAPTER SIX

The Immigration Debate

The debate relating to immigration will always stir up emotion relating to race and national pride. Of course we have seen other nations that have prospered from immigration and Britain too has prospered from the immigration of the '50s and '60s.

Britishness has taken on an ownership dimension for a lot of ethnic minorities where many of them would happily declare themselves to be British and want to be part of the nation by contributing towards the business ethos of this land. The problem we are encountering is adaptability to the enforced immigration that has been inflicted upon the people of this nation; do we really want immigration that does not contribute to this land and its peoples? Some people have said to me, '**Look at the colour of your own skin; how do you dare discuss immigration in a nationalistic manner?**' In Enoch's famous words I normally respond by saying, '**How dare I say such a horrible thing? How dare I stir up trouble and inflame feelings by repeating such a conversation? My answer is that I do not have the right not to do so.**' Of course I have the right to bring up the issue of immigration into my nation; if it is not benefiting our nation, then why I should just surrender my democratic right to discuss an issue that affects my nation's status in a social and economic sense is beyond me. I certainly do not agree with scaremongering amongst the population, but I do agree with tackling immigration that appeases the requirements of the EU and multiculturalists who believe that all is OK and there is nothing to worry about.

The fact that I am of an ethnic minority background has nothing to do with the issue. One can argue that I am from immigrant stock and that Britain gave me the opportunity; there is a difference, and that is the historical and Commonwealth ties. Admission was given to my grandparents and they contributed towards Britain's prosperity; however, they did not intend for the whole of India to follow them. What we have now is a system of non-control and open doors that cannot be closed to allow quality in, rather than quantity with no limits. How can we continue to allow the British people to sit back and just allow tolerance and patience to silence the debate of European immigration? When a nation is being subdued its whole existence of pride gets taken away from it. Democracy loses its rhythm, because the choir are not allowed to sing the chorus but can only lead the song up to it and then listen to someone else singing it for them; **this is not the vision of self-control.**

Areas have changed and the social environment of those areas is contributing to minimum integration. If anyone believes that this statement is not true then the evidence is very clear; many people from the EU have not been able to recognise the efforts that we as a nation have made to improve race relations since the Birmingham speech that Enoch Powell made. We as British and Commonwealth nationals have tried very hard indeed to integrate and eliminate a lot of the prejudices that made life difficult in the '50s, '60s and '70s.

I still believe that many communities that have entered Britain since the fall of communism have found it very difficult to integrate with us because there is no emphasis on understanding Britain before making an entry into our green land. When I make the statement that we have no self-control I mean that we are truly allowing our relationship with the EU to supersede our own values and traditions. One may argue that when Asians came here they too ignored integration and created their own areas, but there was a history with Britain and this country had a strong linguistic relationship with the

West Indies and India. English itself was widely spoken in these places due to the British rule there. We must never forget the strong individual relationship that set up the marriage between India and Britain, and that 'arranged marriage' was created by MK Gandhi and the last Viceroy of India, Lord Mountbatten. By contrast, we were divided from Eastern Europe for many years by the Iron Curtain of communism and we truly had very different views towards freedom and integration. Of course human beings can get on with each other over time but there is something wrong with dominance. My grandparents knew they were coming to a foreign independent land and not a province of Europe. Today we are facing a situation where **'country hopping'** seems to be the norm for many economic migrants and settlement is something that is dictated by economic favourability. Most people of ethnic minority origin came here to settle and contribute towards this land and make it their own home with the intention of integration and not with any emphasis on nation selecting as the economic climate dictated.

Enoch Powell made the statement that areas are changing and that some white people are finding themselves a minority in their own streets. In recent years British children of ethnic minority origin who are now fourth-generation Great British nationals have been finding it hard to have a discussion with other children in school because of cultural and linguistic barriers. There have even been cases where certain children from Eastern Europe have found it difficult to accept our Britishness and to integrate in schools with ethnic minorities. In some larger British cities, ethnic minority teachers who in most cases are third- or fourth-generation Great British have faced racism from these new immigrants coming into Britain.

I was once questioned as a teacher in a Further Education college about my nationality and ability to teach a group of Eastern European women. They insisted on finding out whether I had studied in a European institution and knew of the standards that they expected from me; they completely ignored my Britishness based on the colour of my skin. Some even commented that they felt very strange being taught by someone who is of Indian origin. I have never faced this sort of antipathy from my own British nationals regardless of skin colour. In the light of Enoch Powell's comment that some peoples' lives have been destroyed by the immigration event of the '60s, one has to look at my example to make the comparison; however, reality and scaremongering are two very different issues. My life was not destroyed, but certainly an impact was made and this incident gave me something to think about and discuss.

We are finding that many people of all origins in the United Kingdom who are at least third and fourth generation are asking questions relating to immigration and the worth that it now has. I am a firm believer that Britain satisfied its immigration requirements back in the '60s and what we need now is a firmer approach that leads to quality of immigrant rather than quantity. If people believe that this is an unfair statement then I would like to place this question to them: **is it our responsibility to take on Europe's unskilled and economic migrants?** Of course we are not here to reduce the benefit bill of other nations by taking on their people. I do accept that some want to work and work hard; however, we are paying out in one way or the other and the returns that we are getting are not as fruitful as one would expect.

By being in this union we are also contributing to the '**brain drain**' of other EU nations, mainly from Eastern Europe. Surely there is an impact on other nations like Poland and Lithuania due to their young people leaving; we must be contributing to this problem. At the same time we have many British people who are leaving this nation because they no longer feel part of it. The problems relating to this European integration do not seem to end because people who move always have to start from square one again, thus delaying economic progression.

We cannot sustain this level of immigration that is entering our nation. If we look at race relations, for example, there is surely a problem in having to rearrange our existing relations in the United Kingdom to accommodate this imposed European policy relating to immigration. Unless the people of Britain have a say, there will always be a problem with immigration; the numbers have to be controlled and practical in order for racial and cultural harmony to work within the mechanism of society. If the present trends continue even the ethnic minorities within this nation will become a further minority within minority groups and we may have the American effect where Hispanics overtook the black Americans as being the most disadvantaged in society. My friend who is originally from El Salvador lived in America and he commented on how black people treat Hispanics in America; he made it clear that it did not take long for the racism to reverse and the Hispanics to become the ones who were being terribly discriminated against.

I truly believe that we need a vision that allows us to see the outcome of the future. People state that we cannot see the future and it is wrong to predict, but just have a look at the present trends and examine what can go wrong in the future; safeguarding our interests is not a bad idea to implement.

Britain's interests at present are not being given much regard by the EU. We are different and we are unique in terms of culture, economics and international relations, but we are being forced to surrender our international and national heritage to those who feel we should be part of a United States of Europe. What benefits do we gain from being made to feel as if we are only a segment within a superstate of Europe when we really should be in our driving seat, directing our own destiny within the world in terms of international relations and economic prosperity?

Our minorities are now finding themselves a **minority within a minority** and are being faced with the same challenges that many white people faced when Asians came to this nation. Take my earlier example where people spoke Punjabi in the pub; we are now seeing people like me and other people of ethnic minority origin walking into a pub and hearing Polish or some other Eastern European language being spoken. One may conclude that integration has to take priority to remedy that problem, but when one is faced with a third- or fourth-generation ethnic minority person the likelihood is that English will be their first language. We are now feeling offended when we encounter a language that is totally new to us. We are now finding ourselves to be placed in the social hierarchy by a policy that has been imposed upon us by the EU. The question is this: do British Asian people feel that they are placed in a lower category in the social structure of Britain because the influx of Eastern European immigrants are white and blend in better due to racial characteristics? Or do they feel as if they take priority for helping to rebuild this nation after the war and contribute towards the fields of medicine, commerce and other industries in this nation? Surely someone from a Commonwealth background would have a closer affiliation with the United Kingdom than those who come from an EU nation.

Are the tables truly turning in our nation where it is British Asians who feel that they are Great British and united with white British citizens against the EU and its visible immigration into our land? If we are in the process of social unification against the wave of open-door immigration, we may appear to be aggressive in thought and create antipathy towards a race of people; **that is not the intention and this must not be allowed to develop. We do not want the civil war ethos of Enoch Powell; we want peace.**

On the other hand, what do we do about this situation? In my opinion we need to leave the EU and restore our values and national status. We are British, and that is something we are not willing to negotiate through mass immigration and imposed regulations against our nation. For far too long we have been very tolerant towards the European Union and allowed it to rule our internal affairs. What has greater EU expansion really brought to this nation in terms of prosperity and autonomy? One may argue that we have excellent business links with the EU and we may lose it all if we leave the union; I cannot imagine Angela Merkel convincing the chief executive of Mercedes-Benz not to sell their cars to us in retaliation for us leaving the EU.

We need to be in control of our borders and bring in a system that is fair to the immigrant and to the British national; we cannot continue being the place where everyone wants to come just because they are allowed to come to Britain. We need to restore our values at our border posts and be in control of whom we let in; in my opinion this is not negotiable any longer. If we are scared of the notion that offence will be taken, well, I cannot make an apology for speaking on behalf of the best interests of Britain presently and in the future. We as a nation do not have an issue with races from around the world; we do not have a policy of racial apartheid when we deal with foreign nations; however, overall the present feeling is that our membership of the EU needs to be examined properly. If one were to question stricter immigration rules it would be totally justified to ask interrogative questions to ensure that fairness is applied to immigration policy, but it seems clear that some tougher decisions need to be taken in order for us to restore self-control and have our own autonomy.

How can this be implemented with a tolerant view towards the EU? The answer is that it cannot! If we need control over numbers coming into this nation, we clearly need to be separated from the EU. We also need to have a relationship with the EU that is amicable and allows trade between us and other EU nations; however, we need to remove the shackles that prevent us from making our own decisions. Yes, I sympathise when I speak to the unsure voter or those who live in fear of what may happen if we leave the union, but what do we do: just allow our nation to become a province that must take in the annual flow of immigrants from Europe and agree with the regulations imposed upon it?

To speak in such a tone from an ethnic minority view may well be looked upon as strange, hypocritical or even racist by some quarters. It is not a question of ethnicity but nationality, and for me that clearly is something that stands at the centre of the debate relating to autonomy and independence. Nations are made up of many people, and those who are liberal thinkers must analyse the extent of restrictions that have been imposed upon our liberty. Is it fair that we as a nation must listen to an institution that does not allow us to impose our own rules but feels exceptionally comfortable in taking 11% of our GDP? In 2012 our GDP was roughly £1,560 billion and we paid out 11% of our GDP to the EU; we ended up being approximately £165–£170 billion worse off! Not only are we gagged from a democratic viewpoint, but we also have to pay money to this institution that clearly does not give any value for money. The Office for National Statistics **estimated** the GDP of the UK to be £1,562,263 million in 2012. Take into consideration that this cost is rising each year, and the majority of the British public are not even aware of the fact that so much money is leaving the UK each year to pay for this membership. The only impact that the majority of our citizens are seeing is the immigration crisis that this country is facing through the open-door immigration policy.

Yes, I agree that my views are purely my opinions and thoughts, but I believe in freedom and democracy that allows us to make our decisions and walk a path that is free from interference or political hindrance.

MK Gandhi was a great believer in freedom; he once said, **'To safeguard democracy one must have a keen sense of independence, self-respect and their oneness.'** On another occasion he said, **'Evolution of democracy is not possible if we are not prepared to hear the other side.'**

Britain and its people do not have that sense of independence or oneness; we have found ourselves without the key principles of democracy because, sadly, our previous and present governments have not done a thing to object to

European meddling in our internal affairs. If we truly respected the ethos of governing our own affairs and allowing the British people to have a greater say in the future of this nation, we could clearly relate to the principles of oneness and unity. However, the British people have never truly been treated with democratic respect and independence of choice when it comes to being part of this union. Safeguarding democracy is the responsibility of the government and the people, but sadly the people of this nation never really got a chance to safeguard their interests when it came to European affairs because they were never treated with oneness through official consultation. The critical part of Gandhi's statement is **'one must have a keen sense'**; are the British people keen on political issues relating to the EU, or have they grown fed up and apathetic due to non-consultation by politicians? Have they now lost any faith that this problem can be solved in a way that gives them freedom of expression?

Immigration into Britain has now reached levels of concern for the government; they do not know how to deal with it or how to face the question with an outlook of reaching an amicable conclusion. People can only tolerate so much before they rebel, and at present there is a sense of rebellion in Britain. This will result in a civil approach to dealing with this issue and the values of integrity will remain intact, because the people of this land will not resort to abuse or taking their frustration out on the immigrants by treating them with inappropriate intent.

Enoch Powell once said to a man who approached him, **'Well, why are you depressed? This government will come to an end sooner or later.'** It is a statement that has an element of humour attached to it, but surely, with the way in which the people of this nation are being ignored, they will be the force of change behind choosing a government that will have to deal with the question of the EU. When governments in a democracy do not act in a democratic way, the price they pay will be a heavy one at the ballot box.

We too are now returning to the talk of the '60s; all of us are concerned about the employment prospects of our own children. Why should we not be? We have been born and brought up here in Britain; we are not just going to leave our nation and emigrate. We have invested our interests here in Britain, and most of all we see this green land as our country.

Now people will question my views and ask me to remember what my own grandparents went through when they came here, but I didn't come here; I was born here. The influx of immigration is raising concern amongst the minorities and the white population; we are in this together and we are facing a new challenge to our future. Am I scaremongering? No, I am not scaremongering; I am concerned, because it is inevitable that at present trends of immigration from Europe and in particular Eastern Europe will result in the nationals of this land finding it harder to achieve economic prosperity. Why should anyone question our concerns? As British nationals we have the right to be concerned about the future of our nation, and if we feel that we are being constricted in the employment and economic sense then of course we should raise the question at the highest level.

The concept of integration is questionable when established communities have been nurtured with a long-term integration ethos. The conflict can arise where economic migrants have a short-term view of integration that is determined by economic factors. What will my children think of a Britain where people hop in and hop out as and when they feel like it? I am sure that if this immigration issue is not dealt with our children will be conditioned and just say, 'Oh, well, it has always been like this in the country; it is an EU thing and we just have to go along with it like our parents did.' By that time we will have absolutely no control over our affairs and we truly will be a province within the superstate of Europe. It is not a bad thing to integrate with people and get along in harmony; I totally support integration and getting along in peace with each other. However, there has to be a fair equilibrium and the present state of our nation's immigration issue is threatening that equilibrium.

We initially restricted our immigration policy regarding the former Empire states in 1962; the main bulk of immigrants came to Britain from 1948 to 1962. By that year the immigration from the Commonwealth, largely from India and the West Indies, had already occurred. Governments in the '50s did consider restricting immigration but they did not do so, thus resulting in Enoch's frustration simmering and then reaching boiling point with the Birmingham speech. The governments of the '50s felt it would be wrong in principle to restrict immigration based on a colour bar. The Conservative Home Secretary in the '50s, Sir David Maxwell Fyfe, said, '**Even to contemplate restricting immigration from the colonies would be a step forward towards breaking up the Empire and in other quarters it would regarded in evidence that the government are in favour of a colour bar.**' In 1962 an act was passed limiting immigration; work vouchers came into force and these acted as a control mechanism. However, there was an influx of children and spouses of previous immigrants who wanted to come together again as a family unit, and this was increasing numbers.

Immigration can always be a vote loser for any government; it is essential for any government that they get this issue right, otherwise defeat is inevitable. If we want to create good race relations in Britain we have to restrict the present influx so it is of manageable proportions, otherwise we may find ourselves in a future of uncertainty.

In 1963 Kenya became independent and there were 200,000 British Asian nationals there. Only 20,000 Asians of mainly Indian origin took up the option to become Kenyan nationals, but due to corruption and delays not many got their new Kenyan nationality. The relations between the Asians and the Kenyans were not very good after the Kenyans got their independence; the Asians no longer lived the lifestyle that they had under British rule. Britain could not leave these people stateless, so they had to allow these people to come into Britain and this caused another huge wave of immigration into this country.[1] This caused a lot of issues for the British government at the time; eventually the problem was sorted out, but it had an impact on Britain. This is now history and we have managed to settle in and become British citizens, but one must remember that those British Asians who came from Kenya had a history with Britain and, after all, they were British nationals.

I do favour strong immigration control, but I also favour legislation that prevents discrimination in our country, and sadly this is where Enoch and I differ; he clearly did not want the Race Relations Act to go through because he felt that too much would be given away. Today we are not focusing on race because we have moved on from the race issue; the issue is more about Britain being able to handle the present situation in terms of population, employment prospects for the British citizens and service provision.

In relation to race and the issues that surround it, a poll conducted by Gallup found that public opinion in the late 1960s was at 69% opposing the shadow cabinet for expelling Enoch Powell. Today there is no way the figure would be as high as 69% with the inflammatory language that he used during the Birmingham speech.

I sometimes, like Enoch Powell, find myself having to justify myself against perceptions that I am a racist because of my views on immigration, and I must add that I totally am against racist behaviour. Enoch Powell was once asked the question, **'Is it true that you don't like coloured people, Mr Powell?'** He responded by saying, 'I have very little background of the West Indies and West Indians.' The journalist said, 'That is regrettable, Mr Powell; you talk so much about them.' Enoch replied, **'I can't help it. I have considerable background knowledge of the peoples of India and Pakistan who form three-fifths of all the immigrants; I fell in love with India when I went there and**

---

[1] See www.ibtimes.com/uganda-legacy-idi-amins-expulsion-asians-1972-214289

I have no sense of superiority because of a white skin either to an Indian or West Indian.'

I can relate to Enoch's statement; I do not have a sense of superiority because I am a Great British national, and I do not believe that I should have better rights based just on my nationality and nothing else over a European national. I do not hold such thoughts because of my religious conviction and because of what my nation expects of me, but I do expect my government to act in the interests of all British nationals and to preserve and promote their interests before anyone else's, especially when those who are coming to our nation are making the citizens of this country raise serious questions. Our priority must be Britain and the people who are British, not only in the British Isles but also in our British overseas territories. Some may argue that everyone is entitled to what we grow over in Britain in terms of prosperity, but we too must be entitled to attract whoever we want into Britain in order to prosper and benefit. The relationship of integration must be one of mutual benefit.

The Treaty of Rome that was created in 1957 happened at a time when there were only six nations in the European Community; nobody had envisaged that the ex-communist nations would join us today. The Treaty of Rome related to the free movement of people; we cannot put any restrictions onto this and safeguard our borders because **twenty-eight nations** have to agree to change the Treaty. What chance do we have of making the change that is so necessary for safeguarding our borders when all the rest will undoubtedly not support our claims that we cannot cope with the mass immigration and open-door policy? This proves that we are not in control of our borders and the restrictions that we want to impose cannot happen unless we walk away from the EU and regain our independence.

Before 1962 we could alter by statute, but we cannot do such a thing with the Treaty of Rome. **Clearly this shows we have no control over our borders.** This has nothing to do with the race question as it was back in the '60s, but with Europe we have little chance of negotiating.

Enoch Powell saw Europe as an institution that placed restrictions on our sovereignty as a nation; he made it clear that because of our history of constitutional continuity, we are clearly more aware of what sovereignty actually means than continental nations would be. The principle of self-government meant more than allegiance to a political party; Powell believed in this principle. I would have to agree with him on this issue; the European issue is a case of defence of our sovereignty. We were part of political evolution as a nation; however, the first six were recovering and rebuilding after the war and did not think twice about creating new institutions, something we were not too keen on because of our monarchy, parliamentary system and mature system of government. I believe that from the onset we had little in common with the first six nations of the European Community and this new venture is something we certainly should not have been part of in the first place.

British people have always lived in foreign lands and have contributed towards wealth and prosperity with the knowledge and skills that they exported out of the United Kingdom; this is nothing new and will continue. The issue that we are facing is that we do not have any say over the skills and abilities of the people who are presently coming to Britain. Most people I know are very capable of doing the jobs that many Eastern Europeans do here in the United Kingdom and to be honest there is nothing stopping our people from doing these jobs.

I have engaged in dialogue with many people from the Eastern European nations and they have said that British people do not want the jobs that they do. The question that I would like to ask in a more open domain than just having a chat in a pub or a café is this: how did we survive before these people came to our country, benefiting from the open-door policy that is applicable to those who come from Europe?

If we believe that our people are not capable of doing such jobs then we are very wrong indeed; our people can do these jobs and if required to do so they will do these jobs. The problem is one of greater depth; for the British worker it may be a question of making ends meet with the income that these jobs actually offer. Now this point is crucial because we are not the ones who are nation-hopping; we are here to stay and we have expenses that are greater than those of the people who enter the nation. Many immigrants who come to the UK may not want to buy a home here or feel that they want to settle for a long time, so often their expenses will be very low indeed, particularly in cases of multiple occupancy. Many people have made the comment that a lot of them do not spend their money over here; I can believe this because most of the money is leaving the UK and contributing towards the prosperity of another land in Europe.

Now, a lot of people can counter-attack the statement that I have made, but compare the economic behaviour of present-day European immigrants to that of the original Asian immigrants who came over here in the early days; home ownership is higher amongst the latter group, and the amount of money that is spent on the high streets by these minority groups is generally higher in comparison to those who have come from Europe. One only needs to look at the impact that the East African British Asians made when they came to settle here; a lot of them brought money and, most of all, a business acumen that was excellent for the local economies of places like Leicester. Late-night opening hours were something that did not happen in this nation, but the British Asians from East Africa introduced this hard-working mindset and encouraged local economies to grow. The impact on financial growth made by this initial wave of immigration from the Indian subcontinent and from East Africa was immense. Due to the extended families that Asian people have, especially those from the Indian subcontinent, they have contributed towards higher weekly expenditure in the shops and local towns. What appeared to Enoch to be a disaster turned out to be beneficial to a lot of towns and cities throughout Britain. These people came to settle not as individuals but as families, new Great British families who made this land their home in more ways than just one. Asian weddings alone in this nation are worth over £300,000,000 per annum to the British economy; the average British Asian family can spend up to and over £30,000 on a wedding, whereas their white British counterparts spend 10–13k less (based on 2007 figures). This is not including what they spend on other family functions and celebrations relating to religious and cultural festivals.

We are finding that third- or fourth-generation Asians from the Indian subcontinent do not really have that much left in common with India compared to their grandparents, so their financial focus is firmly in place in Britain. One can argue that Eastern Europeans one day may be like the third- or fourth-generation Asians; there is a possibility, but they are not restricted by immigration controls as the Asians were back in the '60s, so the option of leaving Britain and going to another EU land that is more lucrative is always on the agenda. By contrast, British Asians are obviously firmly fixed in this society and have a different outlook on this country; it is their country and they clearly see it as just that.

There is no doubt that certain cultures have their own work ethic and integration processes that do work. Stereotyping a whole community is wrong and unjust, and I do not support it; however, is it fair to say that in today's Britain we do not judge at all? Of course we do; if we see another community that is new to us, we will want to know something about it. Depending on our social interaction we will look for knowledge, and if our social domain is one of negative vibes towards others then that will colour the image we will create of this new group.

I was once asked if the women in my home walked around with their faces covered and if I had more than one wife. A Polish man asked me these questions because he had previously had no interaction with people from an Asian background and for him this was a new experience. It was only when I met the same man again a few months later that I saw an improvement in his English and an awareness of British Asians; he did admit, though, that he still saw me as an Indian rather than British and that he did not really recognise my nationality. Being assessed on nothing but the colour of one's skin can cause distress, and it is true to say that the person who spoke to me was illiterate with regard to integration because he put my colour before my nationality.

I find it amazing how certain people come from other nations and impose their views upon the ethnic minorities of this nation; these minorities are a very strong part of this nation's fabric, and all of a sudden they are being assessed in a manner that most white British nationals would never attempt. Is it time that we demanded that even EU nationals must pass a British social test before coming here in order to blend and integrate in a better fashion? This is another idea that we cannot implement because it contravenes the rules relating to freedom of movement within the EU. It is all very well subscribing to the views and rules of the EU, but we are finding ourselves being unable to make any laws or rules that demand that EU nationals conform to our way of life or social etiquette. We are powerless to make any changes or even demand that EU nationals adapt to our ways of social interaction; however, our nation's government is very quick to put rules onto non-EU nationals, mainly from the Commonwealth, demanding that they speak English and pass a British residency test. This is unfair; Britain should not treat one foreigner differently from another. It is obvious that someone can come from a European land and not speak a word of English or learn a thing about our values and settle here just because they are European nationals. It is beginning to look very unfair to our Commonwealth, and the EU is in effect making us look discriminatory to the rest of the world.

The flow of immigration into Britain has been excessive in comparison to other trends of immigration. The problem of immigration has taken a new form since the Treaty of Rome, officially the Treaty establishing the European Economic

Community (TEEC), was created by the six nations Belgium, France, Italy, Luxembourg, the Netherlands and West Germany. I have listed figures to highlight the immense scale of EU immigration that we are powerless to deal with. **These numbers from Eastern European nations slowly accelerated after the fall of the Soviet Union in 1991 and increased rapidly with the accession of the Eastern European nations into the EU.**

1881–1914	325,000 Jews entered the UK
1933–1939	50,000 Jews entered the UK from Germany and surrounding nations
1948–1962	250,000 West Indians & Indians from the Indian subcontinent entered the UK
1972	30,000 expelled Ugandan Asians entered the UK
2004	**582,000 immigrants entered the UK (according to records from the BBC News website),**[2] mainly from Eastern European nations such as Poland and the Baltic nations. These immigrants came to the UK in or around 2004 alone. According to the statistics supplied by **Gresham College (fourth lecture on post-war politicians by Vernon Bogdanor – Vernon Bogdanor gave a lecture on Enoch Powell's legacy in British politics)**, however, approximately 1.5 million actually came from Poland and other Eastern European nations in 2004. One can clearly read that there is a discrepancy of just under a million immigrants entering the UK not being accounted for. This may support the claims that European immigration figures are out of control.

The Bogdanor figure of 1.5 million for 2004 probably accelerated from the time Lithuania, Estonia, Poland and Latvia entered the EU. All four countries joined on the 1st May 2004.

---

[2] Casciani, Dominic, 'Record immigration levels to UK' (http://news.bbc.co.uk/1/hi/uk/4359756.stm), BBC News, 20th October 2005, accessed January 2014

However, negotiations with Poland to join the EU had been taking place since 1990. Slovakia became an independent state in 1993 and the UK saw a rise in asylum cases from the Slovak Roma community; Slovakia joined the EU in May 2004 and there has been a huge rise in people from the Roma community in particular who have chosen to settle here. If I were to be asked if I believe that Vernon Bogdanor's figures for in and around 2004 are correct, I would probably agree. However, I do believe that since the fall of communism, before 2004, we have seen a rise in immigration from Eastern Europe; there was certainly a visible presence of Eastern Europeans in the UK in the '90s.

We have recently seen a huge increase in immigration from Eastern Europe into Britain. In comparison to other trends of immigration from the Commonwealth one can clearly see that these figures are immense. Immigration has steadily increased since 2004 on a huge scale. **It is clear that the figure from Eastern Europe is rising on a yearly basis.**

It is obvious that a serious cause of concern in today's politics is the immigration question. The time span from 1881 to 1972 is ninety-one years, and in total over those years the immigration figure was 655,000. In 2004 the figure was 1.5 million with no control over the numbers. **Are we heading towards an immigration crisis that is beyond repair?** I would have to say that the situation can be repaired if we get to grips with the open-door policy and quite simply leave the EU and its grip that is suffocating our self-control.

Certain quarters within the political and media domain believe that the incoming figures since 2004 have been well over 300,000 per annum (according to an EU report prepared by the European commissioner in charge of employment and welfare)[3] and they are set to increase. Can we continue to have

---

[3] Mendick, Robert and Claire Duffin, 'True scale of European immigration' (http://www.telegraph.co.uk/news/worldnews/europe/10375358/True-scale-of-European-immigration.html), *The Telegraph*, 12th October 2013, accessed January 2014

good relations if the numbers are not practical? Can we continue to cope in an economic sense with the pressure put on local authorities and health boards? I do not believe we can continue to manage like this. Many people who show concern over the figures have every right to be worried for the future. If a land is being pressured into accepting something that it does not want, then it is only a matter of time before something has to give. I am aware that there are relationships of friendship and marriage between certain Eastern Europeans and British nationals; however, if we show sympathy to this status then we are trading our emotions for our national interests, and that is a choice that the British government and people have to make with respect to managing uncontrolled 'legal' immigration in the interests of our nation.

We have over 600,000 inactive Eastern Europeans in Britain at present (2013). Does this contribute towards British society? Who is paying for their upkeep here in the United Kingdom? Does the EU help us, considering they have imposed this problem upon us? We are not expected to treat these people any differently to any other British national. I ask why we are allowing this situation to grow; what benefits are we getting from allowing these people to be inactive in our nation?

We are also paying child benefit for over 50,000 children who do not even live in this country. We are paying this money mainly to Eastern European nations. The unrestricted free flow of movement of people from poor to rich nations will cause a heavy burden on those nations perceived as rich. There clearly is more strain on our National Health Service and on local authorities. I am not against anyone who is Eastern European, but this is not fair on the people of our land and it is certainly not fair on the immigrant who is not developing himself or herself or contributing towards Britain in a positive economic sense.

CHAPTER SEVEN

Patriotism

The people of Scotland and Wales in my view have generally always been very patriotic regarding their culture and identity. Obviously Scottish culture is visible through music, dance and of course the reputation for producing good whisky. Many people from England view Scotland as a place to visit for a break or they just see it as a place that is freezing cold; obviously this is a myth.

During the '80s many right-wing groups used football as a platform to pursue their hatred of anything that represented democratic freedom; sadly they used the St George's Cross flag to advertise their presence in a stadium. The Scots did not have such an issue in the cities of Glasgow and Edinburgh; in fact the Scottish flag became something that most if not all Scottish people embraced. It was seen as more cultural and patriotic to display the flag. It gave us a sense of ownership.

I was amazed when I moved to Kent that I hardly saw any English flags around, and I was told that it was because of the offence factor; this truly did throw me overboard. I still cannot fathom why the English in particular do not take ownership of the flag and take pride in displaying it. If people take offence, then that is a problem they have to deal with. England is a part of our nation and I am sure most Scottish football fans would expect to see England fans waving a St George's Cross flag in their faces and vice versa. This is something that has improved in recent years where pubs, schools and other public places do fly the flag and celebrate St George's Day.

It is high time that we discarded the idea that being English is something to be ashamed of because of the football hooligans who desecrated the fabric of that flag. Sadly, most English people accepted political correctness and the hindrances that it brought to this nation; their identity ended up taking a back seat whilst the perception grew from community to community that the flag is something that should be hidden. Why should I expect the Indian government to hide their flag just because they may have people living in their land who are not indigenous Indians? It is absurd to think that they would surrender with so much ease. The Americans certainly do not allow this sort of thing to happen in their nation; in many schools they still sing the national anthem of America before classes start.

Where did we go wrong? Were we far too polite or were we scared of the past, when race relations did take a hammering with racial attacks and the spread of racism in the workplace and schools during the '60s and '70s? We did not know how to embrace the flag properly because we were too busy surrendering to multiculturalism and adopted this **'too scared to offend'** attitude; this has now caused us more problems as the years have passed. I blame the ethos of the multiculturalists for creating this fear factor; it completely distanced our white British citizens by placing a fear in their minds that multiculturalism has been introduced to make the majority feel guilty for the mistakes of the past. I suppose one could say the same about Scottish patriotism; it certainly took a huge leap forward when the movie *Braveheart* was released in this country.

I can agree that history is very valuable for the expansion of knowledge and to feel proud of your nation's achievements, but relevance of the age has to come into the equation. As a British Indian I am very saddened to know that terrible things happened out in India during the Empire, but what can I say to my white British friends? Am I supposed to remind them of the past every day and make them feel guilty for the mistakes of their great-grandparents?

I do feel that it is important for me as a British Indian to feel proud of my nation's achievements and also feel very confident that I can speak about its failures and atrocities of the past. That is what democracy is all about: giving views and opinions that add value to any debate or discussion. If I were to be ignorant of my ethnicity then that would be very wrong of me, because a lot of my thinking and concept of family life comes from India and I cannot change that no matter what I intend to do in life.

Some may say I only go on about Britishness because I am a British national in a legal context; my message to them is that I truly love Britain and its positive heritage in this nation and in the world. Of course when one looks at the colour of my skin the question can be raised of where I am 'from', but if someone were to ask me the question, the answer would firmly be 'the city of Glasgow'. What else am I supposed to say? The city makes up my character, my socialisation, my integration and, most of all, part of my identity. When another Glaswegian person meets me here in Kent or in London, it is always a good opportunity to exchange memories with each other and reminisce about places and people back home in Glasgow. This opportunity returns me to patriotism, and when I see other British people who are also proud of where they come from the opportunity to engage in humorous banter is always there to add a laugh to the conversation.

Patriotism must never be taken for racism, and sadly in our nation this seems to be the 'party spoiler'. It is a terrible shame that if one feels proud of their land they can be at times vilified as being a bigot or someone to avoid. In the public sector workplace it is particularly evident that displays of patriotism are not allowed. I do have an issue with this because when I was in France and Greece I noticed many official buildings like schools and police stations displaying the national flag. I believe that here in the United Kingdom we should do the same; I also believe that all British police forces should have a Union Jack stitched into the shirt, jumper or police high-visibility jacket. I know this statement will cause frustration amongst those who are not so pleased about the displays of patriotism that I have mentioned, but then again what is wrong with them? I am sure in Northern Ireland they would be an issue because of the history and the divide, but we must be practical and embrace what is ours.

I have been to Ebbsfleet train station many times and we have the Police aux Frontières (PAF) there. The PAF are the French immigration police and they are based over here in Kent to check the documents of those who use the Eurostar to go to Paris and beyond. They are very confident in walking on foreign soil with the French flag displayed on their shirts; why are we not? What are we really afraid of? Has anyone ever sat down and asked themselves the question of why there is so much opposition to being patriotic in this green land today?

If this nation does not get a grip on itself sooner or later we will see some solid divisions within it, and that is something that I would not want to see in my lifetime. I do not want this nation to break up. Already we have English people stating that they do not feel British but only English, and we have some Scottish people who want a complete separation from the United Kingdom. I am of the belief that many years of patriotism being left on the shelf and hidden away have resulted in apathy, especially in England. It is very sad that we have reached this stage, but I truly believe this situation can be rectified with days of celebration relating to our Britishness and cultures where all British nationals can engage in events to celebrate being British and what that means. A few public holidays per annum would be very welcome indeed in the summer; I am sure many would agree with me on having more holidays.

We need to salvage Britain and replace a sense of ownership that isn't here amongst us at present. We are allowing divisions to multiply and we have yet to become more cohesive in a social and economic context. Many ethnic minority British people still find it hard to forgive the terrible racism that their grandparents encountered here, and I can fully understand that, but if this is to be our home and our nation we must do something to unite ourselves in order to be one cohesive unit. We cannot hold grudges that hinder our nation's social, domestic and international progress.

In relation to me, all I can say is that I am proud to be an integral part of this nation and I wish to continue to con-tribute towards my society with a positive outlook. My children will have a different view of life depending on how society and Britain as a nation develop in years to come. I only hope that they too will become Great British citizens and feel proud of their place in this nation, regardless of the past errors that politicians and society have made. We can never be totally perfect and there is no way we will be as a society, but if we can become united in a British cultural sense, where people are not categorised based on their ethnicity, we can be unified.

Will we continue to be different? Yes, we will all be different and there is no doubt that I cannot change the colour of my skin, but I can change the way I think and not use the colour of my skin to appeal to the lowest common denominator in order to win an argument or try to get what I want.

There will be people on both sides of the colour spectrum who will feel insecure about doing this. Some are right when they say they feel that they are being discriminated against, because it does happen. However, we cannot be united as a nation if we are segregated from each other in such a way that we allow this insecurity to develop into a hindrance to social interaction. Sadly over the years in our country this has happened and it has taken further years to get to where we are now.

CHAPTER EIGHT

Margaret Thatcher's Swamp

Enoch Powell was not the only politician to discuss immigration from the Commonwealth, although he is normally recognised as the only one who did due to the nature of his speech.

Margaret Thatcher made a comment relating to Britain being 'swamped' by people from the West Indies and the Indian subcontinent. This comment certainly raised a few questions and concerns; whereas previously the debate had been silenced because of Enoch's speech, here it was bubbling on the surface once again. She made the claim that British people were in fear of being swamped by another culture.

This was a statement that was met with a lot of anger in the run-up to the 1979 election. She clearly knew what she was saying because discussing immigration is always an issue of sensitivity and there is no doubt that people want this issue to be dealt with. The use of the word 'swamped' caused concern.

Once again, it has been proven that the Commonwealth immigration has not caused so much concern in this nation as the EU immigration has. I ask the question of why all previous governments and their leaders hid the reality of the EU and what it has now brought to this nation in relation to uncontrolled immigration and expense. It is very easy to talk about Commonwealth immigration in a deliberate attempt to distract attention from the failings of the EU and the implications that these failings have for our nation.

Thatcher did get a lot of support from certain quarters in society relating to her concerns. William Whitelaw, who at the time was the Shadow Foreign Secretary, totally agreed with her regarding the fear of Britain becoming swamped. The word was used in a very calculated manner. Margaret Thatcher was aware of the fact that the National Front only had 2% of the vote in London; however, she was very aware of the potential of these extreme right-wing groups and wanted to ensure that people would vote for a mainstream political party rather than go extreme. She did make it clear in her speech that she did not want the electorate to choose the National Front option, and some may look at her speech as a plea to the voters not to turn to extreme parties for help. This interpretation can be challenged because the National Front was not in any strong political position at the time. The National Front fielded 300 candidates and they all lost their deposits.

I suppose she played a role in damaging the National Front because they were the only party who were really discussing immigration at the time, and I suppose Maggie stole the debate from them and turned it into an opportunity to gain more votes.

In comparison to Enoch's speech, Margaret Thatcher was very mild indeed in the way in which she spoke about the issue. She was not in a temper or angry mood when she made her comments about immigration, and one could easily make the claim that it was not wrong to discuss the issue. However, we must not forget that Enoch's Birmingham speech was only made ten years earlier, so the immigration debate was still a 'touchy' area and anything that had the slightest thing to do with it always stirred up emotion. There were still demonstrations in places like Wolverhampton and other towns and cities; her comments did not cause such an outrage as the Birmingham speech, but there is no doubt that ethnic minorities felt very scared upon hearing the word 'swamped' being used by a politician. There was always going to be a fear factor in society since Enoch made his speech in 1968, and that fear was never going to be eliminated from the hearts and minds of people with ease.

One must remember that at the time of Thatcher's election victory unemployment was a huge problem and the priority was to try to get people back into work as soon as possible. Immigration was therefore a good issue to discuss to ensure that people knew there would not be a new wave of immigration coming into the nation to take jobs. There was a lot more to the comment 'swamped' than just visible numbers of brown and black faces in Britain; it had an economic significance attached to it for those who were white working class and wanted to maintain a sense of security.

We must not forget that Enoch was a Conservative and the comments that Margaret Thatcher made were also from a Conservative viewpoint, so in response the ethnic minority vote would really only go to Labour. There was no way that ethnic minorities would feel safe in voting for Conservatives just because of financial hardship and unemployment; they would vote for a party that made them feel safe in Britain, not unsafe and insecure.

Thatcher stated that people will feel hostile to the numbers of people coming into this nation if there is no control. I can agree with the statement that the numbers have to be practical and I can agree that immigration needs to be discussed, but I cannot agree that Thatcher was clearly speaking in concern for the British people because I truly believe her interests were the interests of business and privatisation. Many people still blame her for destroying the fabric of communities throughout Britain and accuse her of theft relating to the industries that belonged to the state and its people. Immigration was a concern to her but she clearly did not envisage the implications of EU immigration today, because nobody at the time could have guaranteed the collapse of the Soviet Union, which was to give Eastern European nations entry into the United Kingdom. I am sure that if she had had any idea of the state of immigration in today's Britain, she would have had a very different view on the matter.

Thatcher did feel that it would be wrong to give immigrants

council housing and that priority should be given to the white citizens of the country. There was a lot of concern at the time about the Vietnamese boat people and many felt they should be allowed to settle in Britain; she made the comment that those who felt sorry for them must invite them into their own homes. **It goes to show that she was very unsympathetic and ruthless, and if it was not her way then it was no way.** She had fewer objections to Hungarians, Poles and Rhodesians because she believed they could be assimilated more easily into British society. They are still foreigners and that is the bottom line, but it is obvious she was saying that they could be assimilated into this society with greater ease because they could **'blend in'** a lot easier because they were white. She spoke about the nation being swamped by another culture; correct me if I am wrong, but Poles and Hungarians are from a different culture, so how on earth could they, according to Thatcher, be assimilated with greater ease?

Thatcher made it clear that she was not in politics to ignore people's worries but to deal with them. I believe that people in general were mainly worried about how Thatcher would deal with them after seeing her ruthlessness in power.

I must admit in my lifetime I have never come across a British leader who was disliked as much as Margaret Thatcher; the day she resigned I was at college and the celebrations were in full swing within ten minutes of finding out she was no longer Prime Minister.

CHAPTER NINE

Enoch's Legacy and My Place in British Society

Enoch certainly left his mark on British society and there is no doubt he raised the question of race and immigration in a manner that caused controversy.

Has Enoch affected my way of thinking? Yes, he has changed my views in more ways than one and I have become more open-minded than I already was. As a teenager in the '80s and the early part of the '90s I looked upon him as public enemy number one because of his views, but now I am looking at his statements in a very different light.

I am in awe of his views relating to the European issues of concern. I believe he was very right in maintaining the values of this nation and expressing his discontent at what the Heath government was doing back in the '70s. I have become someone who does not believe in being busily engaged in a political union with other nations which do not understand the United Kingdom or its people. I want to be separate. I believe I should be allowed to be a British national without any ties in a political context with the EU; why shouldn't I be? My grandparents came to the United Kingdom of Great Britain and Northern Ireland; they did not come to the United States of Europe.

On the issue of the Birmingham speech, I do believe it was a serious mistake for Enoch Powell to silence the debate on immigration for many years. If he had only used his excellent English speaking skills in a more peaceful manner, I am sure he would have gained political success that could have made him very senior in the British government.

At times I can see where he was coming from; as someone who used to be part of the colonial elite, he obviously still saw himself as part of the ruling class over the natives. He found it very hard to accept that India had become independent and for him this was like a personal loss. However, if Enoch believed that India should not have become independent then what right did he have to believe that Britain should be independent and free from the clutches of Europe? If one believes in freedom then one must not deny others the same right. Then again, there are many in India who complain about the corruption and poverty in the country, resulting in them questioning the substance of their own independence and the sacrifices that were made by so many, like Gandhi, who served prison terms for his beliefs relating to freedom.

Enoch's time was a different time with very different views and I do not believe that he should have been denied the right to express his views or been hidden from the political domain. People like him added to the ethos of democratic views and speech, but we all know there is always a danger that democracy can give birth to a way of thinking that can kill democracy.

As I said, I do question the way in which he made that famous speech; surely he knew of the backlash that would happen and how it could change our society for years to come. However, he was right in discussing restrictions on immigration, and I totally agree with him on this issue. Immigration must be controlled to maintain social equilibrium and avoid lasting effects on a society as a result of dependency on immigration.

He has left me in a position that is not difficult to manage as a British Indian; my integration into British society probably has a lot to do with this. If one fails to integrate it can create problems for the advancement of society overall. I do not believe that Enoch was concerned about the integration issue.

Enoch clearly did not want people coming into this country in the numbers that were arriving on the shores of Britain. We feel the same way today with Eastern European immigration into our country. I get told by many ethnic minorities that we were in the same position at one time ourselves. I do not agree with this statement because it was a different time and age altogether, unlike now when Britain has no control over its immigration and who it allows into this nation. The problem is not so much Commonwealth immigration as it is Eastern European, so there is no doubt the Eastern Europeans will feel that all British nationals regardless of their colour have something against them. I have to disagree. The issue is not about race, like it was back in the '60s and '70s; it is more about managing a problem that could destabilise the social structure of our nation and also cause economic problems for the British state.

Yes, I believe that British people should be looked after by the British state, and as for those who come from Europe and the rest of the world, including our own Commonwealth, they should be allowed to come here only to fill a skills shortage or on a points-based system. If people disagree with this manner of thinking, they really need to look at the figures that are coming into Britain on a yearly basis and decided for themselves what is acceptable and not acceptable. I do not believe that this issue is about race or nationality, but the British people do believe that they must have priority and I cannot see why they must not get priority in jobs, education and most of all prosperity in health and wealth.

We have become very full indeed; Britain is one of the most densely populated places in Europe and there is only so much a nation can handle. If we believe that multiculturalism will come and save the day for this nation, we must be walking on the '**yellow brick road**'; it will not save us but will only allow us to ignore the real issue of immigration and the present problem this nation is facing.

Enoch made the statement that we must be mad to allow in

such an influx of immigrants. If we made ourselves mad I could understand, but the EU is in control of our political mental state and I believe they have made us mad when it comes to dealing with British affairs because it suits them more than us.

I can only sit and await a decision relating to the EU and our future within it. Enoch is now history, but many people are calling him a visionary and stating that he was right all along. He was right to discuss immigration but he did not see the vision that we are watching, which in all essence is purely dictated by the EU. He focused on black and white, whereas the issue is no longer about ethnic minority Commonwealth immigration but mainly about immigration from Eastern Europe. Now it seems that all British nationals are quietly asking questions and raising concerns; it is a bit late for that now. Our tolerance is to blame, and the British voice is being denied a hearing through referenda.

Enoch and I have different outlooks on Britishness and on the question of race relations within our nation; however, there is no doubt we both love Britain and what it means to us as men to be Great British. He was a man of great intellect and there is no doubt that others in Parliament would have avoided getting into a dispute or debate with Enoch Powell relating to immigration or the European question. My only regret is that I never met the man; I am sure we would have managed to discuss many issues other than immigration relating to our great nation. As I come from Glasgow I am sure he would have had some questions for me relating to Scottish independence and I am sure we would have agreed on that question as well, considering that I am opposed to the break-up of our union as a nation.

We as people will always have disputes, but we must remain Great British and civil in dealing with our concerns. This nation can still hold its head up high and regard itself as a positive example that other nations would love to be like in terms of governance and social stability.

We need to leave the European Union and become a nation of integrity and self-rule again if we want to become independent and be in charge of our home. No nation wants to be dominated, and this great nation and its people are no different to others who seek freedom and political independence. I hope that the people of this great nation will one day be able to become self-governing and free again without the interference of Europe in economic and political matters; we are more than capable of dealing with our own affairs. This has been proven over history and hopefully we will once again return democracy, without conditions or interference, to the custodians of Great British democracy: the Great British people who have always been at the centre of the success of this nation.

Passing Indian gentleman